The SURVIVOR'S FAMILY GUIDE

A Resource for Loved Ones After Your Passing

ROBERT W. LUCAS

Success Skills Press

Published by Success Skills Press
Casselberry, Florida 32707 USA

Copyright © 2017 by Robert W. Lucas.

All rights reserved. Printed in the United States of America. Except as permitted under the United States Copyright Law of 1976, no part of this publication may be reproduced or distributed in any form or by any means, electronic or mechanical, including photocopying, recording or otherwise, or stored in a database or retrieval system, without the prior written permission of the copyright owner.

The content of this book contains the sole opinions of the author based on his experience and knowledge as a published author and human resource professional, and should be treated as such. All attempts have been made to ensure that all information, websites, and references contained in this book are correct and accurate at the time of publication. **The content is provided for informational purposes. Neither the author nor the publisher make any warranties or representations related to content, nor do they assume any liability for errors, omissions, or inaccuracies of subject matter contained herein or for damages suffered as a result of content application.** Any incorrect attributions in the book are inadvertent and will be corrected in future editions if notifications are made to the publisher.

This publication is designed to provide accurate and authoritative information in regard to the subject matter covered. It is sold with the understanding that neither the author nor the publisher is engaged in rendering legal, financial planning, accounting, securities trading, or other professional services. If legal advice or other expert assistance is required on the topic areas included, readers are strongly encouraged to seek out the services of competent professionals for guidance and assistance.

Extracted and modified from a Declaration of Principles Jointly Adopted by a Committee of the American Bar Association and a Committee of Publishers and Associations.

Cover and interior design by: Ginger Marks (www.documeantdesigns.com)

Distributed by Robert W. Lucas Enterprises

Library of Congress Control Number: 2016916353

ISBN-13: 978-1-939884-02-2

This book can be printed and customized with your organization's logo if ordered in bulk.

For additional information on printed copies or bulk discounts use the *Order Form* at end of this book or contact:

>Robert W. Lucas Enterprises
>PO Box 180487
>Casselberry, FL 32718-0487 USA
>407-695-5535
>info@robertwlucas.com
>http://www.robertwlucas.com

"What is there to do when people die—people so dear and rare—but bring them back by remembering."

May Sarton

PURPOSE FOR THIS BOOK

This planning guide contains valuable information and my last wishes.

Please use it as a tool to ease the burden of finalizing my estate and preparing to move on with your life.

Printed Name ....
Signature ....
Date ....

As Dr. Spock of the Star Trek movie and television franchise was fond of saying:

"Live long and prosper."

*"The pain passes,
but the beauty remains."*
Pierre Auguste Renoir

CONTENTS

PURPOSE FOR THIS BOOK V
PREFACE XI
A MESSAGE TO THOSE I LOVE XIII
MY FINAL THOUGHTS TO YOU XV

STEPS FOLLOWING MY DEATH 1
  IMMEDIATE NOTIFICATIONS 3
  PEOPLE TO NOTIFY 5
    Family Members to Notify 5
    Other People to Notify 7
    Additional Notifications 9

IMPORTANT INFORMATION YOU WILL NEED 15
  MY VITAL STATISTICS 17
  ITEMS TO GATHER 19

FUNERAL RELATED INFORMATION 25
  ARRANGEMENTS 27
    Funeral/Cremation and Memorial Arrangements 27
    Organ Donation(s) 27
    My Preferred Funeral or Cremation Arrangement Details 28
    Decisions to Make Regarding Funeral/Cremation 35
    Funeral Related Arrangements 36
    Following the Burial/Cremation and Internment 37
    Charitable Donations 37

MONEY MATTERS 39
  STOP OR CHANGE AUTOMATIC PAYMENTS 41
  INCOME SOURCES 44
    Work Income 44
    Non-Traditional Income Sources 45

    Other Income..47
    Money Owed to Me by Others....................................48
    Other Monies Due..51
    Royalties/License Fees..53
    Dividends...55
    Retirement Pay/Pension..56
    Annuities...58

FINANCIAL ACCOUNTS...60
    Personal Bank/Credit Union Accounts*..........................60
    Personal Credit and Debit Cards...............................62

FREQUENT FLYER AND REWARDS PROGRAM ACCOUNTS.................66

OWNED, RENTED, OR LEASED PROPERTY...........................67
ADDITIONAL ASSETS...69
    My Possessions That Others Have...............................69
    Real Estate That I Rent or Lease from Others..................73
    Undeveloped Land that I Own...................................76

VALUABLE POSSESSIONS...79
MODES OF TRANSPORTATION.....................................81
    Cars, Motorcycles, Recreational Vehicles, Planes, etc.........81
RECREATIONAL EQUIPMENT......................................84
    Boats, Jet Skis, Snow Mobiles and Other.......................84
FIREARMS..87
COLLECTABLES..88
    Pictures, Photographs, Statues, and Other Valuable Artwork....88
    Antiques and Heirlooms..91
    Jewelry...94
    Storage Unit(s)...96

INSURANCE CONSIDERATIONS 97
INSURANCE ISSUES 99
Immediate Notifications 99
In Case of Accidental Death or Other Than Natural Causes 99
Other Insurance Issues 100
Insurance Companies 101

MY BUSINESS INFORMATION 103
BUSINESS ESTATE ISSUES 105
Current Business(es)/Organization(s) and Interests 106
    Officers and Key Personnel 107
    Tax Identification Numbers 110
    Bank/Credit Union Accounts 111
    Business Credit/Debit Cards 112
Resources for Business Bookkeeping, Accounting and Tax Preparation . . 115
    Accounting and Bookkeeping 115
BUSINESS ISSUES TO ADDRESS 117
    Creditors 118

TECHNOLOGY RELATED MATTERS 121
SOCIAL MEDIA, INTERNET AND HOME NETWORK . . . 123
Social Media 123

INTERNET 127
WEBSITES 129
Domain Names Owned 129
Website Login Information 129
NETWORK INFORMATION 130
Internet Services 130
Email Settings 131
    Personal Email 131
    Business Email 131
Wireless Router 133

    Broadband Modem 133
    Wireless Network Settings 133

MISCELLANEOUS INFORMATION 135
CARE AND/OR DISPOSITION OF PETS 137
MY TASK LISTING 138
MY SERVICE PROVIDERS 141
    Medical Service Providers 141
    Miscellaneous Service Providers 143

RESOURCES 149
HELPFUL RESOURCES 151
    General Resources 151
    Military Related Resources 156

GENEALOGY 159
FAMILY MEMBERS 161
MY MEMORIES 168

APPENDIX 175
GLOSSARY OF TERMS 177
ADDITIONAL NOTES 185

ABOUT THE AUTHOR 189
BOOKS BY ROBERT W. LUCAS 191
ORDER FORM THE SURVIVOR'S FAMILY GUIDE 193

PREFACE

Depending on one's age, health, religious, cultural values and beliefs, life situation, and perspective, death can be viewed in a number of ways. Some view it with fear and trepidation while others see it as a blessing. No matter what your views on the topic, death is inevitable. Since no one knows when that event will occur, wise and compassionate people take the time to prepare in advance.

Throughout your life, you have likely loved, cared for, and tried to protect those people for whom you are concerned. You can continue to show your caring and support now. In order to help continue to assist your family, friends and loved ones, you can do them a great service by preparing in advance for your own demise. Rather than add trauma and stress to an already emotional life event, why not lighten their load by preparing vital information to aid them in dealing with your passing.

While many people efficiently keep vital records and information throughout their lives, it is often scattered in several locations or not periodically updated. This is especially true related to personal data, legal matters, financial accounts, and related issues.

The Survivor's Family Guide: A Resource for Loved Ones After Your Passing is a designed as an indispensable resource to help family members and others dear to you avoid unnecessary anxiety. By taking a bit of time to collect valuable information and store your last wishes in one handy reference, you give a final gift of love. If you need more pages than provided, make a note to alert your loved one indicating how many additional pages that you created. Then, photocopy blank pages from the book, complete and insert them in to the back when you store the journal.

In this handy planning guide, you will find useful information and a step-by-step journal to record information that will be vital once you are gone. If you take the time to methodically record important data and knowledge, your loved ones will deeply appreciate it once you are no longer here to provide the information or

assist them in gathering it. If any area in the book does not apply to you, put an NA (not applicable) in the blank space. That will prevent your loved one from feeling frustrated or stressed because he or she has to spend time trying to determine whether or not you simply forgot to fill in a section.

An important point to remember is that you should put a note on your calendar each year after you have completed the planning guide. Go back and update anything that has changed so that accurate information is available when it is needed most.

A MESSAGE TO THOSE I LOVE

Dear ....,

No words can tell you how much you have meant to me and the impact you had upon my life. I cherished every moment and event that we shared. Even in difficult times, I appreciated your love, contributions and support. Without it, my life would have been far less fulfilled or manageable. I hope that I returned the love that you deserved and expected and that I brought a degree of happiness into your life.

I have taken time to complete this *The Survivor's Family Guide* because I love you and want to help ensure that you are cared for after I am gone. Even though I am no longer able to be with you, I hope that my efforts give you comfort and help get you through a trying and emotional time. I also encourage you to "pay it forward" by completing a similar guide for those people that you love.

Please do not mourn for me. Celebrate our lives together and do your best to make your own remaining years an opportunity to love others and help make the world a better place. Related to that, I encourage you to seek assistance with matters related to my passing. Ask for help from friends, family, religious, fraternal and other professional sources available to you. I truly want your life to be that of one who is fulfilled.

Please share this message and the contents of this book with our children, my parents, and other members of the family, since my sentiments also apply to them.

My Eternal Love,

Your Signature

"Carve your name on hearts, not tombstones. A legacy is etched into the minds of others and the stories they share about you."
Shannon L. Alder

MY FINAL THOUGHTS TO YOU

Having known me throughout our lives, you likely know my personality and the way I approach life. Now that I am gone, I hope that you will move on with your life and enjoy everything that is available to you. Live, Laugh, Love . . .

Here are some final thoughts and my guidance to you:

....

....

....

....

....

....

....

....

....

....

....

....

STEPS FOLLOWING MY DEATH

IMMEDIATE NOTIFICATIONS

Following my death, there will be many things that must be accomplished to settle my estate. I may have already preplanned or handled a number of these tasks, while others will need to be done immediately following my passing. As you read through this *The Survivor's Family Guide,* you will find the location of important documents and materials, as well as, my wishes and suggestions for handling many of the necessary tasks. You will also find a lot of useful information that will aid you on the emotional journey that you are about to take.

Depending on our the laws in our state law and other legal considerations my will may have to go through the probate process. Consult with my estate's executor or executrix and/or a lawyer to determine next steps to prepare for this possibility.

Some experts encourage you to wait at least six months following the death of a loved one before making any major financial decisions. I urge you to consult the professionals (e.g., certified financial planner or lawyer) that I have mentioned elsewhere in this book before proceeding with such decisions. Do only what you must do to get back to some degree of normalcy in life and then look at making drastic changes or large purchases that you feel are needed.

I suggest that you check each item that you complete off the following list in order to avoid overlooking something.

CRUCIAL: *Arrange for immediate organ/body donations (if I was a donor). Check with a doctor, emergency technicians or coroner to identify local sources. This will probably require transportation of my body to the emergency room to make the donations. A fee for this transport service will likely result.*

- Depending on my situation, immediately contact the hospice nurse, county coroner, or call 911. In the latter instance have a "do-not-resuscitate (DNR or Living Will)" document ready when they get there. Otherwise, they will have to transfer me to the ER to have a doctor pronounce death and an unnecessary medical bill will follow for that service. Do

not move my body from where you find it since there may be questions related to how I died.

- Contact a local close adult family member or friend(s) and ask for their assistance.

- Contact appropriate clergy, religious figure, or spiritual advisor for support, assistance and advice.

- Notify the estate executor or executrix.

PEOPLE TO NOTIFY

FAMILY MEMBERS TO NOTIFY

Here is a listing of close family members that I request that you notify immediately following my death (see **NOTES** section for any additional names not listed below). While these names may be in written address books, contact lists on our computer(s), phone(s) or other electronic device(s), I have listed these people here so that you or an assistant can contact them for me in a timely manner. Some may want to attend any funeral or memorial service to be held in my honor or assist you during a challenging time.

Name/Relationship:

Address: ....

Phone #: ....

Email address: ....

Name/Relationship: ....

Address: ....

Phone #: ....

Email address: ....

Name/Relationship: ....

Address: ....

Phone #: ....

Email address: ....

Name/Relationship: ....

Address: ....

Phone #: ....

Email address: ....

Name/Relationship: ....

Address: ....

Phone #: ....

Email address: ....

Name/Relationship: ....

Address: ....

Phone #: ....

Email address: ....

Name/Relationship: ....

Address: ....

Phone #: ....

Email address: ....

Name/Relationship: ....

Address: ....

Phone #: ....

Email address: ....

OTHER PEOPLE TO NOTIFY

Here is a listing of other family members, friends, business and professional contacts that I would like you to notify of my death (check **NOTES** section for additional names). While these names may be in written address books, contact lists on your computer, phone or other electronic device, I have listed these people here so that you or an assistant can contact them for me in a timely manner. Some may want to attend any funeral or memorial service to be held in my honor.

My Personal Physician: ....

Address: ....

Phone #: ....

Email address: ....

Name/Relationship: ....

Address: ....

Phone #: ....

Email address: ....

Name/Relationship: ....

Address: ....

Phone #: ....

Email address: ....

Name/Relationship: ....

Address: ....

Phone #: ....

Email address: ....

Name/Relationship: ....

Address: ....

Phone #: ....

Email address: ....

Name/Relationship: ....

Address: ....

Phone #: ....

Email address: ....

Name/Relationship: ....

Address: ....

Phone #: ....

Email address: ....

Name/Relationship: ....

Address: ....

Phone #: ....

Email address: ....

Name/Relationship: ....

Address: ....

Phone #: ....

Email address: ....

ADDITIONAL NOTIFICATIONS

As soon as possible following my death, make the following notifications (as appropriate to our situation). If I was a former military member (or a surviving military spouse) and was receiving payments from the military or Veterans Administration, you or my estate executor/executrix will need to contact those organizations to stop payments immediately. This will avoid having to repay the government for overpayments since benefits stop the date of my death.

Contact: My employer(s) (Human Resources)

Reason: Notification of my death, discuss any benefits, COBRA health insurance options, final wages, accrued vacation, insurance and retirement related accounts in place.

Contact Information: ....

....

Contact: My former employer(s) (Human Resources)

Reason: Notification of my death, discuss any life insurance policy I may have had that could be still in effect or might owe you benefits.

Contact Information: ....

....

Contact: My former employer(s) (Human Resources)

Reason: Notification of my death, discuss any life insurance policy I may have had that could be still in effect or might owe you benefits.

Contact Information: ....

....

Contact: My accountant

Reason: Notify of death and begin the process of gathering tax and business data together for closing my estate.

Contact Information: ....

....

People to Notify | 9

Contact: Estate Executor/Executrix
Reason: Notify of death and set up meeting to discuss what needs to be done.

Contact Information: ....

....

Contact: Our family lawyer
Reason: Discuss legal resources available (e.g., estate lawyer, if needed), any nuptial agreements, probate requirements, legal steps to follow.

Contact Information: ....

....

Contact: Bank/Credit Union
Reason: Disposition of funds in saving and checking accounts, paperwork and changes required, safe deposit box, banking and financial account questions. Also, discuss conversion of my credit cards to your name to help establish/enhance your credit rating.

Contact Information: ....

....

Contact: Insurance companies
Reason: Questions about policies, annuities, death benefits, and other related issues.

Contact Information: ....

....

....

....

....

....

Contact: Social Security Administration
Reason: Stop any retirement payment that you and I receive and apply for death benefits.

Contact Information: 800-772-1213; www.sa.gov

Contact: Military branch headquarters, if applicable
Reason: Notify of my death, update dependent ID card and ask about any death benefit or insurance eligibility.

Contact Information: See **RESOURCES** section, for contact information.

Contact: DFAS U.S. Military Annuitant Pay
Reason: Notify of my death, stop retirement payments and inquire about any survivor benefit payments due. Send copy of death certificate.

Contact Information: P.O. Box 7131, London, KY 40742-7131. PH: 800-321-1080 FAX: 800-982-8459; www.dfas.mil/retiredmilitary/forms.html

Contact: Department of Veterans Affairs
Reason: Notify of my death, stop payments that I receive, inquire about any benefits for which you might be eligible and apply for death benefits due on my behalf.

Contact Information: 800-827-1000; www.va.gov

Contact: Office of Personnel Management
Reason: Report the death of a federal retiree or employee, send copy of death certificate and marriage certificate to apply for annuitant benefits.

Contact Information:

Office of Personnel Management, Retirement Operations Center
ATTENTION: Survivor Processing Section, Post Office Box 45, Boyers, Pennsylvania 16017-0045; Phone: 888-767-6738;
https://www.opm.gov/retirement-services/my-annuity-and-benefits/life-events/death/report-of-death/

Contact: U.S. Department of State

Reason: Notify of my death and return my passport for cancellation.

Contact Information: https://travel.state.gov/content/passports/en/passports.html; 877-487-2788

Contact: Mortgage Company

Reason: Change names and update property documentation for each property that I owned, as needed.

Contact Information: ....

....

Contact: Certified Financial Planner

Reason: Investments, retirement funds, planning for monies that you will receive and any questions you have related to financial matters.

Contact Information: See **RESOURCES** section, for resource if we do not currently have a financial planner, or call the number below.

....

Contact: Stock broker

Reason: Discuss what needs to be done with stocks, bonds and other financial instruments that I own.

Contact Information: ....

....

Contact: Electric Company

Reason: Cancel service on any necessary properties or change the name on the account. Inquire about any possible deposit refund due.

Contact Information: ....

....

Contact: Heating Oil Company
Reason: Cancel service on any necessary properties or change the name on the account. Inquire about any possible deposit refund due.

Contact Information: ....

Contact: Water Company
Reason: Cancel service on any necessary properties or change the name on the account. Inquire about any possible deposit refund due.

Contact Information: ....

Contact: Sewer Company
Reason: Cancel service on any necessary properties or change the name on the account. Inquire about any possible deposit refund due.

Contact Information: ....

Contact: Landline Telephone Company
Reason: Cancel service on any necessary properties or change the name on the account. Inquire about any possible deposit refund due.

Contact Information: ....

Contact: Cellphone Company
Reason: Cancel service on any necessary properties or change the name on the account. Inquire about any possible deposit refund due.

Contact Information: ....

Contact: Cable Company

Reason: Cancel service on any necessary properties or change the name on the account. Inquire about any possible deposit refund due.

Contact Information: ....

....

Contact: Internet Provider Company

Reason: Cancel service on any necessary properties or change the name on the account. Inquire about any possible deposit refund due.

Contact Information: ....

....

Contact: ....

Reason: ....

....

Contact Information: ....

....

Contact: ....

Reason: ....

....

Contact Information: ....

....

Contact: ....

Reason: ....

....

Contact Information: ....

....

IMPORTANT INFORMATION YOU WILL NEED

MY VITAL STATISTICS

The following information will likely be useful for your reference at various times in the future. Please check the **NOTES** section at the end of this book for possible additional information about me and my relatives that did not fit into this section.

Full Name (including maiden name): ....

Blood type: ....

Medical conditions: ....

Past operation(s)/date(s): ....

Social Security Number: ....

Military Identification Card#: ....

Birthplace: ....

Birthdate: ....

Citizenship: ....

Permanent address: ....

....

Resided at current address since: ....

....

Home telephone number: ....

Cell phone number: ....

Business phone number: ....

Email address: ....

Current occupation: ....

Current employer: ....

Current employer address: ....

Current employer phone: ....

Religious preference: ....

Veteran (circle one):   Yes   No

Military branch(es): ....

Military serial number: ....

Date(s) of enlistment: ....

Date of final discharge: ....

Type of final discharge: ....

Location at final discharge: ....

Date/place of military retirement: ....

Name/years of conflicts in which served: ....

....

....

....

....

Final rank/Pay grade: ....

NOTES:

ITEMS TO GATHER

The following is important information and documentation that you will need to gather in order to access information, handle my affairs, settle my estate, and make necessary changes. I am providing it to make locating what you need easier for you. There may be other things that you will identify as needed throughout the process of planning my funeral and settling my estate. Check the **NOTES** section for any additional information. If something does not apply, I marked it as NA.

Safe Combination/Location: ....

....
....
....
....
....
....

Estate executor/executrix name/
Contact Information: ....

....
....
....
....
....
....

ITEM	LOCATION
My birth certificate or adoption papers	
Spouse/Significant other birth certificate	
Children's birth certificate(s)	
Adoption records	
Citizenship papers/residence documents	
My Social Security card	
My Medicare card	
My supplemental insurance card	
Your Social Security card	
Social Security Cards of dependent children	
My driver's license	
My passport	
VA benefits ID card (if applicable)	
DD214 (Military discharge papers —if applicable)	
My military/retiree ID card	

ITEM	LOCATION
Union membership cards/documentation	
Marriage certificate(s)	
Pre- or Post-nuptial agreements	
Divorce papers (all previous marriages)	
Medical power of attorney	
Durable power of attorney	
Living Will	
Last Will & Testament	
Safe deposit box key and number	
Life insurance policies	
Health insurance policies	
Annuity plan information	
Stocks/Bonds	
Money market funds/Accounts	
Mortgage(s)/note(s)	

ITEM	LOCATION
Property title(s)	
Notes receivable	
Automobile registration	
Automobile titles/loan documents	
Motor vehicle titles or loan paperwork	
Mutual funds	
Profit sharing information	
Trust information	
Tax Sheltered Annuity Plan (403b) agreements	
Thrift Savings Plan (TSP) agreements	
Certificates of Deposit statements	
401(k) agreements	
Pension plan documents	
Keogh Plan agreements	
SEP agreements	

ITEM	LOCATION
IRA account agreements	
Workers compensation documentation	
Credit/Debit card(s)	
Checkbook	
Savings bonds	
Latest bank/credit union statement(s)	
Preplanned funeral documentation	
Deed to cemetery plot(s)	
Lease/Loan documents (car, boat, RV, property, etc.)	
Motor vehicle, RV, boat, airplane titles or loan paperwork	
Property deeds and titles	
Property tax bills	
Property loan statements	
Unpaid bills	
Contracts	

ITEM	LOCATION
Copies of credit reports from Experian, Equifax and TransUnion	
Car, boat, airplane, RV and equipment keys	
House keys	
Post Office (PO) box key	
Airline frequent flyer/ Reward cards	
Warranties for various household and office items	

FUNERAL RELATED INFORMATION

ARRANGEMENTS

FUNERAL/CREMATION AND MEMORIAL ARRANGEMENTS

If my funeral arrangements or cremation were preplanned, contact the funeral director at the contracted facility below to pick up my body and handle arrangements once I have been pronounced legally dead.

Here is the name/address/contact information for the contracted funeral home/crematory:

....

....

....

If no arrangements have been made, contact one of the following local funeral home or crematories to make arrangements:

....

....

....

ORGAN DONATION(S)

CRUCIAL: Arrange for immediate organ/body donations.

I have initialed all items that pertain and placed an NA in those that do not.

.... I am organ donor and wish to donate the following IMMEDIATELY after my death. Check with a doctor, emergency technicians or coroner to identify local sources. This will likely require transportation of my body to the emergency room.

.... Organs

.... Tissue

.... Entire body

I have arranged for whole body donation to the following organization or medical school.

Organization/Medical School: ....

....

....

Address/Contact: ....

....

....

MY PREFERRED FUNERAL OR CREMATION ARRANGEMENT DETAILS

I <u>have / have not</u> (circle appropriate choice) preplanned my funeral/cremation. In either instance, as a last request, I would like you to include the following initialed items below in any funeral/cremation and memorial ceremony. You can locate alternative sources for caskets, urns, grave markers, memorials and medallions for headstones by searching those terms on an Internet search engine. This can potentially save money. (Please check the **NOTES** section for any possible additional information):

Type of casket (circle one):   Metal   Wood   Fiberglass

.... Casket color: ....
.... Interior color/material: ....

....

.... Casket source: ....

....

....

28 | Funeral Related Information

.... Marker type (circle one):

    Flush ground

    Above ground

    Bronze

    Granite

    Other

.... Marker engraving (described below):

....

....

....

....

....

.... Marker Add-Ons (described below):

    Engraved photo of: ....

....

    Photo location: ....

....

....

.... Military service emblem: (circle one)

    Army

    Navy

    Marine Corps

    Air Force

    Coast Guard

.... Fraternal emblem description:

....

....

....

.... Traditional public casket visitation/viewing.

.... Private funeral/viewing by family and friends only (see **NOTES** section for additional people to invite).

.... Type of burial (circle one):

    Crypt

    Ground space

    Mausoleum

    Cremation niche

.... Internment at cemetery.

.... Plot, mausoleum, crypt location/#: ....

....

.... Cremation with viewing followed by a memorial.

.... Cremation without viewing followed by a memorial.

.... Type of Urn/Source (e.g., custom): ....

....

....

....

.... Type of Urn/Source (e.g., custom): ....

....

....

30 | Funeral Related Information

.... Clergy person/Layperson requested: ....

....

.... Eulogizer requested: ....

....

....

....

.... Place of Service/Memorial: ....

....

....

.... Participating Organization(s) (e.g., military, fraternal, etc.): ....

....

....

............Military type honors (if entitled):   YES   NO

............Flag: YES   NO

............Clothing to be worn (e.g., suit/dress, favorite clothes, military, law enforcement, fire fighter or other uniform) described below:

....

....

....

....

.... Remove medals or insignia from uniform before burial / cremation (circle one)

YES NO

............Give to: ....

Arrangements | 31

............Names/contact information of pallbearers requested:

....
....
....
....
....
....
....
....
....
....
....
....
....
....
....
....
....

............Jewelry (circle one)

    Leave on

    Return to family

............Glasses (circle one)

    Leave on

    Remove (donate)

Music to Be Played (e.g., favorite songs):

Activities (e.g., read a special poem, religious verse, or book passage, or facilitate a group activity with attendees):

Obituary Content:

....

....

....

....

....

....

....

....

....

....

....

....

....

....

....

Additional Special Requests (e.g., flower types, donations in lieu of flowers, photo of me [and others] displayed, military salute ceremony, memorial instead of funeral, location/time of any memorial, reminder gifts distributed to attendees, or programs with details of the funeral/memorial). See **NOTES** section for potential additional information:

....

....

....

....

....

DECISIONS TO MAKE REGARDING FUNERAL/CREMATION

Once you select a funeral/crematory facility, you can choose to use their services to arrange for the following of your choice (if I have not indicated a preference above):

- Decide type of processing (e.g., traditional funeral or cremation).
- Sign necessary documents.
- Burial site selection (if cremation followed by scattering of ashes will not take place).
- Vault or crypt.
- Casket/Urn selection.
- Outer burial vault or grave liner.
- Order headstone and engraving.
- Location of funeral service and/or memorial.
- Funeral transportation.
- Condolences book to collect attendee names (if desired).
- Clothing in which I will be dressed.
- Select person to conduct service/deliver eulogy.
- Order flowers (unless charitable donations will be suggested as an alternative).
- Select music to be used at funeral or memorial.
- Select pallbearers.
- Place obituary.
- Order copies of death certificate within 10 days (some sources suggest at least 10-15 copies that will be needed for various organizations, agencies and purposes).

- Arrange for streamed and/or recorded service for people who cannot make the service/memorial (if funeral home offers this service).

FUNERAL RELATED ARRANGEMENTS

In addition to the actual funeral/memorial arrangements, there are quite a few associated things that typically have to be covered by the spouse/significant other or family members or friends.

- Notify my employer (if applicable) to see what benefits are in place and if life insurance exists. If so, find out how to apply for them.

- Contact a trust and estates attorney to assist with transfer of assets and probate issues (if you do not already have one).

- Notify our accountant or tax preparer for guidance on filing.

- Notify family, friends, military, fraternal, religious and professional associates.

- Arrange lodging and transportation for out-of-town funeral/memorial attendees.

- Select clothing that spouse/significant other and children will wear to the funeral/memorial.

- Plan to greet visitors and family at home (e.g., those staying in the family home and those coming after the ceremony to pay condolences).

- Greet attendees at the funeral/memorial.

- Arrange childcare for infants or disabled children not attending the ceremony/memorial.

- Arrange care/assistance for elder family members dependent on spouse or significant other.

- Arrange to have one of my photos enlarged to use in any planned memorial.

- Keep a list of people who contact you to pay condolences, send flowers, or donations.

FOLLOWING THE BURIAL/CREMATION AND INTERNMENT

- Check with county or city Clerk of Court to get guidance on probate requirements. If there is an Executor or Executrix of the estate, he/she would normally handle this.

- Depending on what the Clerk of Court tells you, make a list of my personal property (not jointly owned assets) that will possibly be part of the probate process.

CHARITABLE DONATIONS

Contact charitable organization(s) to make donations of clothing, glasses, hearing aids, assistive devices/medical equipment and other items. See **HELPFUL RESOURCES** section, for some possible charitable sources.

"Mourning is one of the most profound human experiences that it is possible to have . . . The deep capacity to weep for the loss of a loved one and to continue to treasure the memory of that loss is one our noblest human traits."

Edwin S. Shneidman

MONEY MATTERS

STOP OR CHANGE AUTOMATIC PAYMENTS

Change or cancel the following automatic account billings paid from my checking, savings, credit union or credit cards accounts. These might include credit card, utility, mortgage, loans, subscriptions, trade and fraternal organizations, automobile clubs, sorority/fraternity, alumni associations, or gym. Check with the bank and credit union listed in the **HELPFUL RESOURCES** section, to find out what payments need to be stopped before my accounts are transferred to your name or closed.

Payee/Contact: ....

Account type: ....

Due date: ....

Paid from: ....

User name: .... Password: ....

Payee/Contact: ....

Account type: ....

Due date: ....

Paid from: ....

User name: .... Password: ....

Payee/Contact: ....

Account type: ....

Due date: ....

Paid from: ....

User name: .... Password: ....

Payee/Contact: ....

Account type: ....

Due date: ....

Paid from: ....

User name: .... Password: ....

Payee/Contact: ....

Account type: ....

Due date: ....

Paid from: ....

User name: .... Password: ....

Payee/Contact: ....

Account type: ....

Due date: ....

Paid from: ....

User name: .... Password: ....

Payee/Contact: ....

Account type: ....

Due date: ....

Paid from: ....

User name: .... Password: ....

Payee/Contact: ....

Account type: ....

Due date: ....

Paid from: ....

User name: .... Password: ....

Payee/Contact: ....

Account type: ....

Due date: ....

Paid from: ....

User name: .... Password: ....

Payee/Contact: ....

Account type: ....

Due date: ....

Paid from: ....

User name: .... Password: ....

Payee/Contact: ....

Account type: ....

Due date: ....

Paid from: ....

User name: .... Password: ....

INCOME SOURCES

This section details a financial picture showing my current and future sources of income, savings, credit, insurance and other related revenue streams, as well as, my valuable possessions.

WORK INCOME

The following sources provide full and part time income and might include active military reserves participation.

Employer: ....

Human Resources/Manager: ....

Address/Phone number: ....

....

Pay cycle (e.g., weekly, bi-weekly, monthly): ....

Hours per week/month: ....

Salary per pay period/Annual income: ....

Employer: ....

Human Resources/Manager: ....

Address/Phone number: ....

....

Pay cycle (e.g., weekly, bi-weekly, monthly): ....

Hours per week/month: ....

Salary per pay period/Annual income: ....

Employer: ....

Human Resources/Manager: ....

Address/Phone number: ....

....

Pay cycle (e.g., weekly, bi-weekly, monthly): ....

Hours per week/month: ....

Salary per pay period/Annual income: ....

Employer: ....

Human Resources/Manager: ....

Address/Phone number: ....

....

Pay cycle (e.g., weekly, bi-weekly, monthly): ....

Hours per week/month: ....

Salary per pay period/Annual income: ....

NON-TRADITIONAL INCOME SOURCES

The following sources provide income from more non-traditional sources (e.g., article writing, speeches, online advertising commissions, such as, Amazon, Commission Junction or Google), online auction sales (e.g., eBay), and website product sales.

Source: ....

Payer: ....

Contact: ....

Address/Phone#/Email: ....

....

Income Sources | 45

Account/payee#: ....

Pay cycle/dates: ....

Range of payments per cycle: ....

Where deposited: ....

Source: ....

Payer: ....

Contact: ....

Address/Phone#/Email: ....

....

Account/payee#: ....

Pay cycle/dates: ....

Range of payments per cycle: ....

Where deposited: ....

Source: ....

Payer: ....

Contact: ....

Address/Phone#/Email: ....

....

Account/payee#: ....

Pay cycle/dates: ....

Range of payments per cycle: ....

Where deposited: ....

OTHER INCOME

Payment type: ....

Payer: ....

Amount: ....

Due date: ....

Where deposited: ....

Payment type: ....

Payer: ....

Amount: ....

Due date: ....

Where deposited: ....

Payment type: ....

Payer: ....

Amount: ....

Due date: ....

Where deposited: ....

Payment type: ....

Payer: ....

Amount: ....

Due date: ....

Where deposited: ....

MONEY OWED TO ME BY OTHERS

The following monies owed to me by other individuals or organizations (e.g., recent items sold or loans).

Name of Individual or Organization Debtor: ....

....

....

Debtor Contact Information: ....

....

....

Location of Documentation/Papers: ....

....

....

Details: ....

....

....

....

Amount: ....

Due date: ....

....

Notes:

Name of Individual or Organization Debtor: ....

....

....

Debtor Contact Information: ....

....

....

Location of Documentation/Papers: ....

....

....

Details: ....

....

....

....

Amount: ....

Due date: ....

....

Notes:

Name of Individual or Organization Debtor: ....
....
....

Debtor Contact Information: ....
....
....

Location of Documentation/Papers: ....
....
....

Details: ....
....
....

Amount: ....
Due date: ....
....

Notes:

OTHER MONIES DUE

The following is a list of monies owed to me for various reasons (e.g., lottery payouts or judgements awarded to me).

Contact Name/Information: ....

....

Description/Details: ....

....

....

Contact Name/Information: ....

....

....

Description/Details: ....

....

....

Contact Name/Information: ....

....

....

Description/Details: ....

....

....

Contact Name/Information: ....

....

Description/Details: ....

....

....

Income Sources | 51

Contact Name/Information: ....
....
....
Description/Details: ....
....
....

Contact Name/Information: ....
....
....
Description/Details: ....
....
....

Contact Name/Information: ....
....
....
Description/Details: ....
....
....

Contact Name/Information: ....
....
....
Description/Details: ....
....
....

ROYALTIES/LICENSE FEES

I earn the following income from book, art, music or other types of royalties paid based on sales or licensing of my intellectual and artistic properties.

Source: ....

Payer: ....

Contact: ....

Address/Phone#/Email: ....

....

....

....

Account/Payee: ....

....

Pay cycle/Dates: ....

Range of payments per cycle: ....

Where deposited: ....

....

Location of Agreements/Contracts: ....

....

....

Notes:

Source: ....

Payer: ....

Contact: ....

Address/Phone#/Email: ....

....

....

....

Account/Payee: ....

....

Pay cycle/Dates: ....

Range of payments per cycle: ....

Where deposited: ....

....

Location of Agreements/Contracts: ....

....

....

Notes:

DIVIDENDS

Source: ....

    Address/Phone#/Email: ....

....

....

....

Account#: ....

Pay cycle/Dates: ....

Range of payments per cycle: ....

Where deposited: ....

Location of stock certificates: ....

....

....

Source: ....

    Address/Phone#/Email: ....

....

....

....

Account#: ....

Pay cycle/Dates: ....

Range of payments per cycle: ....

Where deposited: ....

Location of stock certificates: ....

....

Source: ....

Address/Phone#/Email: ....

....

....

....

Account#: ....

Pay cycle/Dates: ....

Range of payments per cycle: ....

Where deposited: ....

Location of stock certificates: ....

....

....

RETIREMENT PAY/PENSION

Here is a listing of my current and/or pending retirement income sources.

Payment type: ....

Payer: ....

Address/Phone#/Email: ....

....

....

....

Payment due date: .... Payment amount: ....

Where deposited: ....

Location of stock certificates: ....

....

56 | Money Matters

Payment type: ....

Payer: ....

Address/Phone#/Email: ....

....

....

....

Payment due date: .... Payment amount: ....

Where deposited: ....

Location of stock certificates: ....

....

....

Payment type: ....

Payer: ....

Address/Phone#/Email: ....

....

....

....

Payment due date: .... Payment amount: ....

Where deposited: ....

Location of stock certificates: ....

....

ANNUITIES

These are annuities that I have in place that are currently paying monies or are scheduled to in the future.

Source: ....

Address/Phone#/Email: ....

....

....

....

Payment due date: .... Payment amount: ....

Where deposited: ....

....

Source: ....

Address/Phone#/Email: ....

....

....

....

Payment due date: .... Payment amount: ....

Where deposited: ....

....

58 | Money Matters

Source: ....

Address/Phone#/Email: ....

....

....

....

Payment due date: ....Payment amount: ....

Where deposited: ....

....

Source: ....

Address/Phone#/Email: ....

....

....

....

Payment due date: ....Payment amount: ....

Where deposited: ....

....

Source: ....

Address/Phone#/Email: ....

....

....

....

Payment due date: ....Payment amount: ....

Where deposited: ....

....

FINANCIAL ACCOUNTS

PERSONAL BANK/CREDIT UNION ACCOUNTS*

The following information pertains to my financial accounts. If I have additional bank or credit union accounts, it can be found in the *NOTES* section.

Related to this list, keep all bank and credit union statements and correspondence, including date stamped envelopes until after my estate has been completely settled. They may be needed as documentation or proof in case issues or questions arise.

*Note: See Business Section for business related banking information

Name/address of bank/Credit union: ....

....

....

Bank/Credit Union phone number: ....

Type of account(s): ....

Account number(s): ....

User Name: ....

Password: .... PIN: ....

Name/address of bank/Credit union: ....

....

....

Bank/Credit Union phone number: ....

Type of account(s): ....

Account number(s): ....

User Name: ....

Password: .... PIN: ....

Name/address of bank/Credit union: ....

....

....

Bank/Credit Union phone number: ....

Type of account(s): ....

Account number(s): ....

User Name: ....

Password: ....PIN: ....

Name/address of bank/Credit union: ....

....

....

Bank/Credit Union phone number: ....

Type of account(s): ....

Account number(s): ....

User Name: ....

Password: ....PIN: ....

Name/address of bank/Credit union: ....

....

....

Bank/Credit Union phone number: ....

Type of account(s): ....

Account number(s): ....

User Name: ....

Password: ....PIN: ....

PERSONAL CREDIT AND DEBIT CARDS

Here is a list of all the personal credit and debit cards that I have in my name (check the **NOTES** section for any additional cards that I might have). Order copies of my three credit reports (see the **HELPFUL RESOURCES** section in the back of this book for credit reporting agency contact information). You are entitled to a free copy of each companies report through www.AnnualCreditReport.com.

Cross- check the following list against credit reports to ensure I did not forget any accounts. Also, notify each credit reporting company of my death to put a freeze on my accounts so that no one can apply for credit in my name.

Type of card (circle one):

      MC   VISA   AmEx   Discover   Other

Issuing company: ....

Address/Phone#/Website: ....

Account number: ....

User Name: ....

Password: .... PIN: ....

Type of card (circle one):

      MC   VISA   AmEx   Discover   Other

Issuing company: ....

Address/Phone#/Website: ....

Account number: ....

User Name: ....

Password: .... PIN: ....

Type of card (circle one):

    MC   VISA   AmEx   Discover   Other

Issuing company: ....

Address/Phone#/Website: ....

Account number: ....

User Name: ....

Password: ....PIN: ....

Type of card (circle one):

    MC   VISA   AmEx   Discover   Other

Issuing company: ....

Address/Phone#/Website: ....

Account number: ....

User Name: ....

Password: ....PIN: ....

Type of card (circle one):

    MC   VISA   AmEx   Discover   Other

Issuing company: ....

Address/Phone#/Website: ....

Account number: ....

User Name: ....

Password: ....PIN: ....

Type of card (circle one):

      MC   VISA   AmEx   Discover   Other

Issuing company: ....

Address/Phone#/Website: ....

Account number: ....

User Name: ....

Password: .... PIN: ....

Type of card (circle one):

      MC   VISA   AmEx   Discover   Other

Issuing company: ....

Address/Phone#/Website: ....

Account number: ....

User Name: ....

Password: .... PIN: ....

Type of card (circle one):

      MC   VISA   AmEx   Discover   Other

Issuing company: ....

Address/Phone#/Website: ....

Account number: ....

User Name: ....

Password: .... PIN: ....

Type of card (circle one):

    MC   VISA   AmEx   Discover   Other

Issuing company: ....

Address/Phone#/Website: ....

Account number: ....

User Name: ....

Password: .... PIN: ....

Type of card (circle one):

    MC   VISA   AmEx   Discover   Other

Issuing company: ....

Address/Phone#/Website: ....

Account number: ....

User Name: ....

Password: .... PIN: ....

Type of card (circle one):

    MC   VISA   AmEx   Discover   Other

Issuing company: ....

Address/Phone#/Website: ....

Account number: ....

User Name: ....

Password: .... PIN: ....

FREQUENT FLYER AND REWARDS PROGRAM ACCOUNTS

Like many people I signed up for frequent flyer and rewards programs with airlines, credit card companies, stores and other companies and organizations. My accumulated points have monetary value and some may allow transfer of points to the account of you or another beneficiary. Check with each of the companies below to determine point accumulations that might exist.

Type of account: ....

Company/Organization: ....

Address/Phone#/Website: ....

Name on account: ....

Account number: ....

User Name: ....

Password: .... PIN: ....

Type of account: ....

Company/Organization: ....

Address/Phone#/Website: ....

Name on account: ....

Account number: ....

User Name: ....

Password: .... PIN: ....

OWNED, RENTED, OR LEASED PROPERTY

ADDITIONAL ASSETS

MY POSSESSIONS THAT OTHERS HAVE

The following items belong to me, but are currently in the possession of someone else at present.

Person holding: ....

Contact information: ....

....

Details: ....

....

....

Person holding: ....

Contact information: ....

....

....

Details: ....

....

....

Person holding: ....

Contact information: ....

....

....

Details: ....

....

REAL ESTATE THAT I OWN

The following is a listing of buildings and other real estate that I own.

Type of real estate: ....

Financed through/Owned by: ....

Finance address/Phone#: ....

....

....

Co-owned by/Contact#: ....

....

Property location/Address: ....

....

....

Use (Rental/lease or personal occupancy): ....

Beneficiary: ....

Estimated value: ....

Type of real estate: ....

Financed through/Owned by: ....

Finance address/Phone#: ....

....

....

Co-owned by/Contact#: ....

....

Property location/Address: ....

....

Use (Rental/lease or personal occupancy): ....

Beneficiary: ....

Estimated value: ....

Type of real estate: ....

Financed through/Owned by: ....

Finance address/Phone#: ....

....

....

Co-owned by/Contact#: ....

....

Property location/Address: ....

....

....

Use (Rental/lease or personal occupancy): ....

Beneficiary: ....

Estimated value: ....

Type of real estate: ....

Financed through/Owned by: ....

Finance address/Phone#: ....

....

....

Co-owned by/Contact#: ....

....

Property location/Address: ....

....

....

Use (Rental/lease or personal occupancy): ....

Beneficiary: ....

Estimated value: ....

Type of real estate: ....

Financed through/Owned by: ....

Finance address/Phone#: ....

....

....

Co-owned by/Contact#: ....

....

Property location/Address: ....

....

....

Use (Rental/lease or personal occupancy): ....

Beneficiary: ....

Estimated value: ....

REAL ESTATE THAT I RENT OR LEASE FROM OTHERS

I rent or lease to following buildings from others.

Type of real estate: ....

Property address: ....

....

....

Use: ....

....

....

Rented/Leased from/Phone#: ....

....

....

Monthly rent/Lease price: ....

Contract/Agreement expiration date: ....

Key location or entrance code: ....

Security alarm code: ....

Additional Assets | 73

Type of real estate: ....

Property address: ....

....

....

Use: ....

....

....

Rented/Leased from/Phone#: ....

....

....

Monthly rent/Lease price: ....

Contract/Agreement expiration date: ....

Key location or entrance code: ....

Security alarm code: ....

Type of real estate: ....

Property address: ....

....

....

Use: ....

....

....

Rented/Leased from/Phone#: ....

....

....

Monthly rent/Lease price: ....

Contract/Agreement expiration date: ....

Key location or entrance code: ....

Security alarm code: ....

Type of real estate: ....

Property address: ....

....

....

Use: ....

....

....

Rented/Leased from/Phone#: ....

....

....

Monthly rent/Lease price: ....

Contract/Agreement expiration date: ....

Key location or entrance code: ....

Security alarm code: ....

UNDEVELOPED LAND THAT I OWN

I own the following empty lots or rural acreage.

Co-owner(s) Contact: ....
....
....

Finance company/Contact: ....
....

Geographic location: ....
....
....

Plot#: ....
Description: ....
....
....

Deed location: ....
Key location or entrance code: ....
Leased to/Contact: ....
....
Lease location: ....
....
....
....

Co-owner(s) Contact: ....

....

....

Finance company/Contact: ....

....

Geographic location: ....

....

....

Plot#: ....

Description: ....

....

....

Deed location: ....

Key location or entrance code: ....

Leased to/Contact: ....

....

Lease location: ....

....

....

....

"We must embrace pain and burn it as fuel for our journey."
Kenji Miyazawa

VALUABLE POSSESSIONS

MODES OF TRANSPORTATION

CARS, MOTORCYCLES, RECREATIONAL VEHICLES, PLANES, ETC.

I own or lease the following vehicles. See **NOTES** section at the end of this book for possible additional items.

Type: ....

Description

      Year: .... Make: ....

      Color: .... Model: ....

Vehicle Identification # (VIN): ....

License tag#/State: ....

Financed/Leased through/Contact#: ....

....

Co-owned by/Contact#: ....

Property location: ....

....

Insured through/Contact: ....

....

Key location: ....

Notes:

Type: ....

Description

    Year: ....Make: ....

    Color: ....Model: ....

Vehicle Identification # (VIN): ....

License tag#/State: ....

Financed/Leased through/Contact#: ....

....

Co-owned by/Contact#: ....

Property location: ....

....

Insured through/Contact: ....

....

Key location: ....

Notes:

Type: ....

Description

    Year: ....Make: ....

    Color: ....Model: ....

Vehicle Identification # (VIN): ....

License tag#/State: ....

Financed/Leased through/Contact#: ....

....

Co-owned by/Contact#: ....

Property location: ....
....

Insured through/Contact: ....
....

Key location: ....
Notes:

Description

      Year: ....Make: ....

      Color: ....Model: ....

Vehicle Identification # (VIN): ....

License tag#/State: ....

Financed/Leased through/Contact#: ....
....

Co-owned by/Contact#: ....

Property location: ....
....

Insured through/Contact: ....
....

Key location: ....
Notes:

Modes of Transportation | 83

RECREATIONAL EQUIPMENT

BOATS, JET SKIS, SNOW MOBILES AND OTHER

Here are the boats, jet skis, snow mobiles, and other recreational equipment that I own.

Type: ....

Description

       Year: ....Make: ....

       Color: ....Model: ....

Vehicle Identification # (VIN): ....

License tag#/State: ....

Financed/Leased through/Contact#: ....

....

Co-owned by/Contact#: ....

Property location: ....

....

Insured through/Contact: ....

....

Key location: ....

Notes:

84 | Valuable Possessions

Type: ....

Description

    Year: .... Make: ....

    Color: .... Model: ....

Vehicle Identification # (VIN): ....

License tag#/State: ....

Financed/Leased through/Contact#: ....

....

Co-owned by/Contact#: ....

Property location: ....

....

Insured through/Contact: ....

....

Key location: ....

Notes:

Type: ....

Description

     Year: .... Make: ....

     Color: .... Model: ....

Vehicle Identification # (VIN): ....

License tag#/State: ....

Financed/Leased through/Contact#: ....
....

Co-owned by/Contact#: ....

Property location: ....
....

Insured through/Contact: ....
....

Key location: ....

Notes:

FIREARMS

Make/Model/Caliber: ....

....

Serial#: ....

Location: ....

Beneficiary/Contact: ....

....

Estimated value: ....

Make/Model/Caliber: ....

....

Serial#: ....

Location: ....

Beneficiary/Contact: ....

....

Estimated value: ....

Make/Model/Caliber: ....

....

Serial#: ....

Location: ....

Beneficiary/Contact: ....

....

Estimated value: ....

COLLECTABLES

PICTURES, PHOTOGRAPHS, STATUES, AND OTHER VALUABLE ARTWORK

Following is a list or valuable art items that I own or co-own.

Item: ....

Description: ....

....

Co-owned by/Contact#: ....

....

Location: ....

....

Estimated value: ....

Item: ....

Description: ....

....

Co-owned by/Contact#: ....

....

Location: ....

....

Estimated value: ....

Item: ....

Description: ....

....

Co-owned by/Contact#: ....

....

Location: ....

....

Estimated value: ....

Item: ....

Description: ....

....

Co-owned by/Contact#: ....

....

Location: ....

....

Estimated value: ....

Item: ....

Description: ....

....

Co-owned by/Contact#: ....

....

Location: ....

....

Estimated value: ....

Item: ....

Description: ....

....

Co-owned by/Contact#: ....

....

Location: ....

....

Estimated value: ....

Item: ....

Description: ....

....

Co-owned by/Contact#: ....

....

Location: ....

....

Estimated value: ....

Item: ....

Description: ....

....

Co-owned by/Contact#: ....

....

Location: ....

....

Estimated value: ....

ANTIQUES AND HEIRLOOMS

The following is a list of antiques and family heirlooms that I own or co-own.

Item: ....

Description: ....

....

Co-owned by/Contact#: ....

....

Location: ....

....

Estimated value: ....

Item: ....

Description: ....

....

Co-owned by/Contact#: ....

....

Location: ....

....

Estimated value: ....

Item: ....

Description: ....

....

Co-owned by/Contact#: ....

....

Location: ....

....

Estimated value: ....

Item: ....

Description: ....

....

Co-owned by/Contact#: ....

....

Location: ....

....

Estimated value: ....

Item: ....

Description: ....

....

Co-owned by/Contact#: ....

....

Location: ....

....

Estimated value: ....

Item: ....

Description: ....

....

Co-owned by/Contact#: ....

....

Location: ....

....

Estimated value: ....

Item: ....

Description: ....

....

Co-owned by/Contact#: ....

....

Location: ....

....

Estimated value: ....

Item: ....

Description: ....

....

Co-owned by/Contact#: ....

....

Location: ....

....

Estimated value: ....

JEWELRY

This is the jewelry that I own. Check the *Notes* section for additional items.

Item: ....

Description: ....

....

Location: ....

....

Estimated value: ....

Item: ....

Description: ....

....

Location: ....

....

Estimated value: ....

Item: ....

Description: ....

....

Location: ....

....

Estimated value: ....

Item: ....

Description: ....

....

Location: ....

....

Estimated value: ....

Item: ....

Description: ....

....

Location: ....

....

Estimated value: ....

Item: ....

Description: ....

....

Location: ....

....

Estimated value: ....

Item: ....

Description: ....

....

Location: ....

....

Estimated value: ....

STORAGE UNIT(S)

In addition to the property I have listed in this book, I also have additional property in the following storage units. Here is the information you need to access it.

Storage Company: ....

Telephone: ....

Email: ....

Address & Unit#: ....

....

Key location: ....

Lease expiration date: ....

Lease location: ....

Additional Information: ....

....

Storage Company: ....

Telephone: ....

Email: ....

Address & Unit#: ....

....

Key location: ....

Lease expiration date: ....

Lease location: ....

Additional Information: ....

....

INSURANCE CONSIDERATIONS

INSURANCE ISSUES

IMMEDIATE NOTIFICATIONS

As soon as possible, reach out to the following companies or organizations. The **HELPFUL RESOURCES** section in this book has contact information to help locate some of these.

All personal insurance companies (e.g., life, health, home mortgage) through which I have some type of insurance to get claims forms.

Veterans Group Life Insurance (if I was on active duty, in the active reserves, or had insurance through the Veterans Administration).

All of my credit card issuers, banks, credit unions, and savings and loan organizations (see the **FINANCIAL** section of this book for a listing). Check to see if you are due any death insurance payments due from these organizations related to credit cards, loans or mortgages. Also, discuss conversion of any credit cards in my name to yours to help establish or expand your credit.

IN CASE OF ACCIDENTAL DEATH OR OTHER THAN NATURAL CAUSES

Obtain any police reports that might be related to my death.

Contact insurance company that we use for our homeowners, automobile or other applicable policies for guidance and forms related to possible claims.

Identify insurance companies for any party that might have contributed to my death (e.g., vehicle driver, public transportation, governmental entities, manufacturers, or other type or organization).

If my death was caused by negligence on the part of another individual or organization, contact a liability lawyer. Search the Internet, ask others for recommendations, or contact the American Bar Association (see **HELPFUL RESOURCES** section) to identify a competent, bar certified lawyer.

OTHER INSURANCE ISSUES

If I had annuity plans, check to find out what benefits you will receive and what steps you have to take to transfer the accounts (see **IMPORTANT INFORMATION YOU WILL NEED** section for contacts).

Keep all insurance related mail and documents until the all estate matters are resolved. Even if premium payments were stopped, a policy might still be in force or have value. Date stamped mail envelopes can be proof of payment or correspondence with an insurance company if issues arise.

Save copies of my obituary. Some insurance companies may require it to verify my death and burial.

Collect all receipts, invoices and other documents related to funeral and estate costs for possible use when submitting claims for various types of insurance payments. These will also be useful during any required probate process.

If I have business enterprises, and it is closed or sold, cancel any business related insurance policies (e.g., Errors and Omissions or other liability coverage) and also cancel any umbrella policies that might be related to it that are attached my homeowners policy. Check with my bookkeeper or in any bookkeeping software that is used for the company to determine insurance coverage and source(s).

Check with my fraternal organizations to see if there is any insurance, death or spousal benefits or assistance available (see **HELPFUL RESOURCES** in back of this book).

To ensure that there are no additional insurance policies in effect for me, you can pay a fee to the MIB Group to do a search at http://www.mib.com/lost_life_insurance.html.

Search my (and your) name and company name(s) on the government website http://www.missingmoney.com to ensure that there is no unclaimed property or money due us.

You can also contact The National Association of Insurance Commissioners (NAIC) https://eapps.naic.org/life-policy-locator/ for assistance in searching for policies.

Check with my current and former employers to determine if I had any life insurance policies with them and if you are due any benefits (see the **HELPFUL RESOURCES** section in the back of this book for names and contact information).

Check with my current employer within 30 days of my death regarding health insurance that I had for myself and the family. You are entitled to assume that policy and pay for it under the federal government Consolidated Omnibus Budget Reconciliation Act (COBRA) for up to eighteen months (see **PEOPLE TO CONTACT—ADDITIONAL NOTIFICATIONS** section).

INSURANCE COMPANIES

The following are insurance companies with which I have policies and/or annuities.

Company: ....

Contact Information: ....

....

Policy#: ....

Company: ....

Contact Information: ....

....

Policy#: ....

Company: ....

Contact Information: ....

....

Policy#: ....

Company: ....

Contact Information: ....

....

Policy#: ....

Company: ....

Contact Information: ....

....

Policy#: ....

Company: ....

Contact Information: ....

....

Policy#: ....

Company: ....

Contact Information: ....

....

Policy#: ....

Company: ....

Contact Information: ....

....

Policy#: ....

Company: ....

Contact Information: ....

....

Policy#: ....

MY BUSINESS INFORMATION

BUSINESS ESTATE ISSUES

This section addresses points to consider if I owned or had interest in one or more companies or organizations. There are many things to do when selling or closing down a business or organization. If I had a business lawyer, financial planner and accountant, contact them immediately for guidance and assistance in making appropriate notifications and filing necessary paperwork to sell or close the business. If those professionals are not in place, ask friends, relatives and other personal contacts for recommendations. You can also do an Internet search to find local resources to assist you. The Executor/Executrix designated in my will might be able to assist with this process.

Another possible source for lawyers is the State Bar Association (normally in the Capital) for a listing of qualified and certified lawyers in the area. You can check the State Bar Associations listing at http://www.statebarassociations.org/.

For a listing of certified public accountants, check out the National Association of State Boards of Accountancy at https://nasba.org/stateboards/ to find the board in our state and then reach out to them for a list of possible professionals.

Keep in mind that many aspects of the business have potential value. Some of these include customer contact listings, products, equipment, website domain names, trademark/company name, and intellectual property (e.g., models, products or publications that I or the company developed).

You can find useful information related to closing a business on the U.S. Small Business Administration's website https://www.sba.gov/managing-business/closing-down-your-business/steps-closing-business.

CURRENT BUSINESS(ES)/ORGANIZATION(S) AND INTERESTS

The following are businesses that I own or in which I have a business interest as an investor or active participant.

Business/Organization Name: ....

Address/Phone#: ....

....

....

My Role/Interest: ....

....

Business Documentation Location: ....

....

Business/Organization Name: ....

Address/Phone#: ....

....

....

My Role/Interest: ....

....

Business Documentation Location: ....

....

Business/Organization Name: ....

Address/Phone#: ....

....

....

My Role/Interest: ....

....

Business Documentation Location: ....

....

Business/Organization Name: ....

Address/Phone#: ....

....

....

My Role/Interest: ....

....

Business Documentation Location: ....

....

OFFICERS AND KEY PERSONNEL

Following is a list of key personnel and decision makers in my business interests.

Business/Organization: ....

Employee: ....

....

....

Position/Title: ....

Phone: .... Email: ....

Business Estate Issues | 107

Business/Organization: ....

Employee: ....

....

....

Position/Title: ....

Phone: ....Email: ....

Business/Organization: ....

Employee: ....

....

....

Position/Title: ....

Phone: ....Email: ....

Business/Organization: ....

Employee: ....

....

....

Position/Title: ....

Phone: ....Email: ....

Business/Organization: ....

Employee: ....

....

....

Position/Title: ....

Phone: ....Email: ....

Business/Organization: ....

Employee: ....

....

....

Position/Title: ....

Phone: .... Email: ....

Business/Organization: ....

Employee: ....

....

....

Position/Title: ....

Phone: .... Email: ....

Business/Organization: ....

Employee: ....

....

....

Position/Title: ....

Phone: .... Email: ....

TAX IDENTIFICATION NUMBERS

Following are tax identification numbers for each of the business entities that I own. Notifications related to changes to the business (e.g., change of ownership, sale, or closing) must be made to the Internal Revenue Service (see **HELPFUL RESOURCES** section in the back of this book) and to the State licensing and taxation entity where the business or organization is located.

Business/Organization: ....

State: ....

Federal tax ID# (EIN/Social Security#): ....

State tax ID#: ....

State license/tax contact website: ....

....

State resale sales tax certificate#: ....

Expiration date: ....

Business License#: ....

Expiration date: ....

Registered Agent: ....

Contact Name: ....

Phone: ....

Website: ....

User Name: .... Password: ....

Dun & Bradstreet#: ....

Website: ....

User Name: .... Password: ....

BANK/CREDIT UNION ACCOUNTS

The following information pertains to my financial accounts. If I have additional bank/credit union accounts, the information can be found in the **NOTES** section.

Related to this list, keep all bank and credit union statements and correspondence, including date stamped envelopes until after my estate has been completely settled. They may be needed as documentation or proof in case issues arise.

Name/address of bank/Credit union: ....

....

....

Bank/Credit Union phone number: ....

Type of account(s): ....

Account number(s): ....

User Name: ....

Password: .... PIN: ....

Name/address of bank/Credit union: ....

....

....

Bank/Credit Union phone number: ....

Type of account(s): ....

Account number(s): ....

User Name: ....

Password: .... PIN: ....

Name/address of bank/Credit union: ....

....

....

Bank/Credit Union phone number: ....

Type of account(s): ....

Account number(s): ....

User Name: ....

Password: .... PIN: ....

Name/address of bank/Credit union: ....

....

....

Bank/Credit Union phone number: ....

Type of account(s): ....

Account number(s): ....

User Name: ....

Password: .... PIN: ....

BUSINESS CREDIT/DEBIT CARDS

Here is a list of all the business credit and debit cards that I have in my name. Order copies of my three credit reports (see the **HELPFUL RESOURCES** section in the back of this book for credit reporting agency contact information). You are entitled to a free copy of each companies report through www.AnnualCreditReport.com.

Cross- check the following list against credit reports to ensure I did not forget any accounts. Notify each reporting company of my death to put a freeze on my accounts so that no one can apply for credit in my name or that of my company/organization.

Type of card (circle one):

    MC   VISA   AmEx   Discover   Other

Issuing company: ....

Address/Phone#/Website: ....

Account number: ....

User Name: ....

Password: .... Pin: ....

Type of card (circle one):

    MC   VISA   AmEx   Discover   Other

Issuing company: ....

Address/Phone#/Website: ....

Account number: ....

User Name: ....

Password: .... Pin: ....

Type of card (circle one):

    MC   VISA   AmEx   Discover   Other

Issuing company: ....

Address/Phone#/Website: ....

Account number: ....

User Name: ....

Password: .... Pin: ....

Type of card (circle one):

    MC   VISA   AmEx   Discover   Other

Issuing company: ....

Address/Phone#/Website: ....

Account number: ....

User Name: ....

Password: ....Pin: ....

Type of card (circle one):

    MC   VISA   AmEx   Discover   Other

Issuing company: ....

Address/Phone#/Website: ....

Account number: ....

User Name: ....

Password: ....Pin: ....

Type of card (circle one):

    MC   VISA   AmEx   Discover   Other

Issuing company: ....

Address/Phone#/Website: ....

Account number: ....

User Name: ....

Password: ....Pin: ....

Type of card (circle one):

MC   VISA   AmEx   Discover   Other

Issuing company: ....

Address/Phone#/Website: ....

Account number: ....

User Name: ....

Password: .... Pin: ....

RESOURCES FOR BUSINESS BOOKKEEPING, ACCOUNTING AND TAX PREPARATION

ACCOUNTING AND BOOKKEEPING

I use the following resources or software to track customers, accounts, creditors, products, services, invoice, and handle other aspects of bookkeeping, accounting and tax preparation.

Accountant/CPA: ....

Phone: ....

Address: ....

....

Account number/ID: ....

Bookkeeper: ....

Phone: ....

Address: ....

....

Accounting software: ....

User Name: ....

Password: .... Pin: ....

Additional Financial Resource:

BUSINESS ISSUES TO ADDRESS

The following is a partial listing of issues that must be dealt with related to my business before settling my estate and dealing with any necessary probate issues:

- Contact all creditors to notify of the death and closing/sale of the company. Arrange for payment of any outstanding invoices from my estate.

- Check my bookkeeping/accounting software and/or check with my bookkeeper (below) as listed in the **RESOURCES FOR BUSINESS BOOKKEEPING, ACCOUNTING AND TAX PREPARATION** section, to determine if there are any outstanding customer invoices that have receipts due. Follow-up on those to collect monies owed.

....
....
....
....
....
....
....
....
....
....
....
....
....
....
....

CREDITORS

The following is a partial listing of my usual business creditors. Ensure that they are all notified of my death and paid monies due. Check my bookkeeping software and contact my bookkeeper to determine if there are outstanding invoices and to coordinate accounts payment.

Creditor: ....

Account#: ....

Address: ....

....

Phone#: ....

Email: ....

Creditor: ....

Account#: ....

Address: ....

....

Phone#: ....

Email: ....

Creditor: ....

Account#: ....

Address: ....

....

Phone#: ....

Email: ....

Creditor: ....

Account#: ....

Address: ....

....

Phone#: ....

Email: ....

Creditor: ....

Account#: ....

Address: ....

....

Phone#: ....

Email: ....

Creditor: ....

Account#: ....

Address: ....

....

Phone#: ....

Email: ....

Creditor: ....

Account#: ....

Address: ....

....

Phone#: ....

Email: ....

Creditor: ....

Account#: ....

Address: ....

....

Phone#: ....

Email: ....

Creditor: ....

Account#: ....

Address: ....

....

Phone#: ....

Email: ....

Creditor: ....

Account#: ....

Address: ....

....

Phone#: ....

Email: ....

Creditor: ....

Account#: ....

Address: ....

....

Phone#: ....

Email: ....

TECHNOLOGY RELATED MATTERS

SOCIAL MEDIA, INTERNET AND HOME NETWORK

SOCIAL MEDIA

You (or someone else) will need to close my online and social media accounts, blogs and personal website (unless there is a financial or other reason to keep my websites open). You will likely need to produce a power of attorney and provide a copy of my death certificate to accomplish this due to privacy laws. Please post one final message on each site (as appropriate) to let followers, friends, and acquaintances of my death prior to closing each account. See the *NOTES* section at the end of this book for possible additional social media accounts and websites that would note fit into this section.

Website hosting company:

Hosting Website: ....

Phone#: ....

Account#/email: ....

User Name: .... Password: ....

My personal website:

Domain: ....

User Name: .... Password: ....

Business website:

Domain: ....

User Name: .... Password: ....

Facebook:

Domain: ....

User Name: .... Password: ....

LinkedIn:

Domain: ....

User Name: .... Password: ....

Pinterest:

Domain: ....

User Name: .... Password: ....

Twitter:

Domain: ....

User Name: .... Password: ....

Instagram:

Domain: ....

User Name: .... Password: ....

YouTube:

Domain: ....

User Name: .... Password: ....

Google+:

Domain: ....

User Name: .... Password: ....

WhatsApp:

Domain: ....

User Name: .... Password: ....

Snapchat:

Domain: ....

User Name: .... Password: ....

Flickr:

Domain: ....

User Name: .... Password: ....

Additional accounts not previously listed:

....

....

....

....

....

....

....

....

....

....

....

....

....

....

....

....

....

....

"It takes strength to make your way through grief, to grab hold of life and let it pull you forward."

Patti Davis

INTERNET

WEBSITES

DOMAIN NAMES OWNED

I have additional website domain names that I purchased, but have yet to use. These are "parked" (not currently being used for websites or blogs) on the following domain registrar websites. You or someone who is knowledgeable about website domains should contact these registrars and find out how to put these domains up for auction (unless you would like to use them or transfer them to a family member or friend). Some may be worth money. Check the *NOTES* section in the back of this book for possible additional domain names owned.

Domain Registrar (e.g., GoDaddy, Name.com, etc.)

Name: ....

Website: ....

User Name: .... Password: ....

Phone number: ....

WEBSITE LOGIN INFORMATION

In a world where data security is a crucial part of online existence, I likely have many websites that I (or my company) own or to which I subscribe (e.g., as a member, follower, or subscriber). Being able to access, change or shut down my blogs, business, social, professional and other accounts will be an important part of my estate closure. Here are the user names and passwords for all my personal and business accounts (see *NOTES* section for other possible sites not listed in this section).

Website name/Domain: ....

Control Panel URL: ....

User Name: .... Password: ....

Database Password: ....

WordPress Domain: ....

Admin Control Panel URL: ....

User Name: .... Password: ....

NETWORK INFORMATION

This section contains technical information related to my Internet service, home network and email accounts.

INTERNET SERVICES

Internet provider company name: ....

Internet Service Provider (ISP) #: ....

Account number: ....

Phone# or Email associated with account: ....

Customer service#: ....

Technical support number: ....

Notes:

EMAIL SETTINGS

PERSONAL EMAIL

Email address: ....

Password: ....

Incoming mail server type: ....

Incoming server: ....

Incoming server port#: ....

Outgoing server: ....

Outgoing server port#: ....

Email address: ....

Password: ....

Incoming mail server type: ....

Incoming server: ....

Incoming server port#: ....

Outgoing server: ....

Outgoing server port#: ....

BUSINESS EMAIL

Email address: ....

Password: ....

Incoming mail server type: ....

Incoming server: ....

Incoming server port#: ....

Outgoing server: ....

Outgoing server port#: ....

Email address: ....

Password: ....

Incoming mail server type: ....

Incoming server: ....

Incoming server port#: ....

Outgoing server: ....

Outgoing server port#: ....

Email address: ....

Password: ....

Incoming mail server type: ....

Incoming server: ....

Incoming server port#: ....

Outgoing server: ....

Outgoing server port#: ....

Email address: ....

Password: ....

Incoming mail server type: ....

Incoming server: ....

Incoming server port#: ....

Outgoing server: ....

Outgoing server port#: ....

WIRELESS ROUTER

Brand: ....

Model: ....

Serial number: ....

Admin URL/IP address: ....

User Name: .... Password: ....

BROADBAND MODEM

Model: ....

Media Access Control (MAC) address: ....

Serial number: ....

Admin URL/IP address: ....

Password: ....

WIRELESS NETWORK SETTINGS

Service Set Identifier (SSID): ....

W-Fi Protected Access (WPA) password/key: ....

Wired Equivalent Privacy (WEP) Password: ....

Serial number: ....

Admin URL/IP address: ....

User Name: .... Password: ....

Notes:

"Grief does not simply go away. It must be chased by the memories of a love departed and a desire to move on."

Robert W. Lucas

MISCELLANEOUS INFORMATION

CARE AND/OR DISPOSITION OF PETS

As you may know, I consider our/my pets to be part of the family. As such, I request that you treat them with the same love and care that I provided. If you cannot or do not want to continue taking care of them, I request that you find a loving adoptive home for them. There may be funding provided in my Will for this purpose. Please check that document before taking any action concerning the pets.

....

....

....

....

....

....

....

....

....

....

....

....

....

....

....

....

MY TASK LISTING

Over time you and I have shared many roles and household chores. In many instances I may have not recognized how important your efforts were in helping make the household run more efficiently and effectively. For that, I apologize. I really did appreciate all the small things that you did to make our daily lives more comfortable and less stressful.

I too took care of little day-to-day tasks (e.g., taking out the trash, cutting the grass, washing the car(s), helping cleaning the bathroom, etc.) and wanted to highlight them here. Not to gloat or point out "look what I did," but to help remind you of a need to get them done and ease your transition as you decide news ways to deal with these extra tasks. As with other items outlined in this book, I encourage you to enlist the help of others where possible. This will ease your burden and take trivial responsibilities off your schedule.

Day of the Week: ....

Task: ....

How I Do It: ....

....

....

....

....

....

....

....

Day of the Week: ....

Task: ....

How I Do It: ....

....

....

....

....

....

....

....

Day of the Week: ....

Task: ....

How I Do It: ....

....

....

....

....

....

....

....

....

....

Day of the Week: ....

Task: ....

How I Do It: ....

....

....

....

....

Day of the Week: ....

Task: ....

How I Do It: ....

....

....

....

....

....

....

....

MY SERVICE PROVIDERS

The following is a list of people and organizations that I have patronized and used for a variety of products and services. I trust these providers and encourage you to consider continuing usage. Obviously, you are free to select resources with which you feel comfortable or that are more conveniently located. This list is purely to inform and take one more task off your to do list.

MEDICAL SERVICE PROVIDERS

General Practitioner

Provider: ....

Address: ....

Phone#: ....

Specialist Practitioner: ....

Provider: ....

Address: ....

Phone#: ....

Specialist Practitioner: ....

Provider: ....

Address: ....

Phone#: ....

Specialist Practitioner: ....

Provider: ....

Address: ....

Phone#: ....

Optometrist: Eye glasses/exams

Provider: ....

Address: ....

Phone#: ....

Ophthalmologist

Provider: ....

Address: ....

Phone#: ....

Dentist

Provider: ....

Address: ....

Phone#: ....

Orthodontist

Provider: ....

Address: ....

Phone#: ....

Audiologist

Provider: ....

Address: ....

Phone#: ....

Additional Service Providers

Provider: ....

Address: ....

Phone#: ....

Provider: ....

Address: ....

Phone#: ....

Provider: ....

Address: ....

Phone#: ....

Provider: ....

Address: ....

Phone#: ....

MISCELLANEOUS SERVICE PROVIDERS

The following is a list of additional service providers that I regularly use for various functions.

Gardener/Lawn care

Provider: ....

Address: ....

Phone#: ....

Pool maintenance

Provider: ....

Address: ....

Phone#: ....

Pest management

Provider: ....

Address: ....

Phone#: ....

Home cleaning

Provider: ....

Address: ....

Phone#: ....

Snow removal

Provider: ....

Address: ....

Phone#: ....

Home repairs/Odd jobs

Provider: ....

Address: ....

Phone#: ....

Sprinkler repair

Provider: ....

Address: ....

Phone#: ....

Plumber

Provider: ....

Address: ....

Phone#: ....

Electrician

Provider: ....

Address: ....

Phone#: ....

Computer maintenance

Provider: ....

Address: ....

Phone#: ....

Computer (IT) support

Provider: ....

Address: ....

Phone#: ....

Automobile maintenance

Provider: ....

Address: ....

Phone#: ....

Car detailing

Provider: ....

Address: ....

Phone#: ....

Shopping assistant

Provider: ....

Address: ....

Phone#: ....

Medical transportation

Provider: ....

Address: ....

Phone#: ....

Meal preparation

Provider: ....

Address: ....

Phone#: ....

Hair stylist/Barber

Provider: ....

Address: ....

Phone#: ....

Nail technician

Provider: ....

Address: ....

Phone#: ....

Personal trainer

Provider: ....

Address: ....

Phone#: ....

Pet sitter/Dog walker

Provider: ....

Address: ....

Phone#: ....

House sitter

Provider: ....

Address: ....

Phone#: ....

Miscellaneous Service providers

Provider: ....

Address: ....

Phone#: ....

Provider: ....

Address: ....

Phone#: ....

Provider: ....

Address: ....

Phone#: ....

Provider: ....

Address: ....

Phone#: ....

Provider: ....

Address: ....

Phone#: ....

"Love is a fabric which never fades, no matter how often it is washed in the water of adversity and grief."
Robert Fulghum

RESOURCES

HELPFUL RESOURCES

The following table of helpful resources should save you time looking up information that can assist in finalizing preparations before and after my funeral or cremation. These sources can provide information and services that will aid you in locating people and organizations that can handle various important functions regarding settling my estate and preparing for the probate process, if that is required in our state.

In some instances the information is available at the websites and phone numbers I have identified and may require someone reaching out to these people or organizations. In other instances, I have researched local resources for national groups and listed their contact information here to save you time and trouble. There may be additional listings in the **NOTES** section in the back of this book.

GENERAL RESOURCES

The following table contains the names and contact information for resources that I believe will be useful immediately to you following my death and in the future.

SOURCE	PURPOSE	ADDRESS	PHONE	WEBSITE
AARP	Grief & loss Information	601 E Street, NW Washington DC 20049	888-687-2277	http://www.aarp.org/home-family/caregiving/grief-and-loss/
American Bar Association	Listing of state bar associations to find an estate lawyer			www.abanet.org
Annual Credit Report	Source for one free credit report a year from each of the three credit reporting companies			www.annualcreditreport.com

SOURCE	PURPOSE	ADDRESS	PHONE	WEBSITE
My Bank	Change names on accounts, cancel credit cards and other financial issues.			
Big Brother/Big Sisters	Clothing, vehicle, furniture, office equipment donations			www.bbbs.org
Cell Phones for Soldiers	Donations of old cell phones to allow military personnel without phones to make calls home			www.cellphonesforsoldiers.com
Consumer Reports	What to Do When a Loved One Dies	101 Truman Avenue Yonkers, NY 10703	800-333-0663	http://www.consumerreports.org/cro/magazine/2012/10/what-to-do-when-a-loved-one-dies/index.htm
My Credit Union	Change names on accounts, cancel credit cards and other financial issues.			
Donate Life	Organ, eye & tissue donation	701 East Byrd Street, 16th Floor, Richmond, VA 23219	804-377-3580	https://www.donatelife.net/
Dress for Success	Donations of professional women's clothing	32 East 31st St, New York, NY 10016	212-532-1922	www.dressforsuccess.org

152 | Resources

SOURCE	PURPOSE	ADDRESS	PHONE	WEBSITE
Equifax Credit Agency	Credit report and death notifications	P.O. Box 740241 Atlanta, GA 30374		http://www.equifax.com
Experian Credit Agency	Credit reports and death notifications	P.O. Box 9701, Allen, TX 75013	888- 397- 3742	http://www.experian.com/
Eye Bank Assn of America	Eye and cornea donation	1015 18th St NW Ste 1010, Washington, DC 20036	202-775-4999	http://restoresight.org/
Federal Employees Group Life Insurance	Employee and retiree insurance assistance	1900 E Street, NW, Washington, DC 20415	202-606-1800	https://www.opm.gov/healthcare-insurance/life-insurance
Florence Isaacs Blogs	Advice on funerals, grief and related topics			http://www.florenceisaacs.com/blogs.html
Federal Trade Commission	Shopping for Funeral Services	600 Pennsylvania Avenue, NW Washington, DC 20580	202-326-2222	https://www.consumer.ftc.gov/articles/0070-shopping-funeral-services
Goodwill Industries	Source for list of local chapters that accept donations			www.goodwill.org
Internal Revenue Services	Deceased persons – probate, filing estate & individual taxes		800-829-1040	https://www.irs.gov/businesses/small-businesses-self-employed/deceased-taxpayers-probate-filing-estate-and-individual-returns-paying-taxes-due
My Primary Care Physician	Medical records/ assistance			

Helpful Resources | 153

SOURCE	PURPOSE	ADDRESS	PHONE	WEBSITE
National Association of State Boards of Accountancy	List of Certified Public Accountants by state			https://nasba.org/stateboards/
National Institute on Aging	Things to do after someone dies	Building 31, Room 5C27 31 Center Dr, MSC 2292 Bethesda, MD 20892	800-222-2225	https://www.nia.nih.gov/health/publication/end-life-helping-comfort-and-care/things-do-after-someone-dies
Salvation Army	Listing of local Salvation Army locations for donations			www.salvationarmyusa.org
Social Security Administration	How social security can help when a family member dies	1100 West High Rise 6401 Security Blvd. Baltimore, MD 21235	800-772-1213	https://www.ssa.gov/pubs/EN-05-10008.pdf
State Bar Associations	Listing of state bar associations to locate local lawyers who are bar certified			http://www.statebarassociations.org/
State business licensing office	This is the entity that registered and licenses businesses in our state			
TransUnion Credit Agency	Credit report request and death notifications	P.O. Box 105281 Atlanta, GA 30348-5281	877-322-8228	http://www.transunion.com/customer-support/contact-us

154 | Resources

SOURCE	PURPOSE	ADDRESS	PHONE	WEBSITE
Union Contact	Information about death and other survivor benefits related to my union membership			
United Network of Organ Sharing	Organ, eye & tissue donation	700 N. 4th Street Richmond, VA 23219	804-782-4800	https://www.unos.org/
U.S. Department of the Treasury	Savings bonds and Treasury notes		844-284-2676	https://www.treasurydirect.gov/indiv/research/indepth/ebonds/res_e_bonds_eedeath.htm
U.S. Small Business Administration	Steps to Closing a Business	409 3rd St, SW Washington DC 20416	800-827-5722	https://www.sba.gov/managing-business/closing-down-your-business/steps-closing-business
Vitalrec.com	Source for listings of state offices to obtain marriage, divorce, birth, death certificates			http://www.vitalrec.com/
WikiHow	How to acquire a death certificate			http://www.wikihow.com/Acquire-a-Death-Certificate

MILITARY RELATED RESOURCES

If I served on active or reserve duty with any branch of the military or the National Guard, please check with the following sources to make appropriate notifications and access any benefits due to me and you. If I died as a result of military service, check with the VA for spousal and children benefits (e.g., college education) that might be available.

SOURCE	PURPOSE	ADDRESS	PHONE	WEBSITE
Air Force Retiree Services	Information about reporting a death and benefits			http://www.retirees.af.mil/About-Us/SBP/
American Legion	Membership questions and notification of death of member	700 N. Pennsylvania St, PO Box 1055, Indianapolis, IN 46206	800-433-3318	http://www.legion.org/contact
Coast Guard Retiree Services	Information about benefits			http://www.uscg.mil/retiree/
Defense Financing & Accounting System (DFAS)	Active & retired military pay issues & questions	DFAS-IN/Debt and Claims Dept. 3300 ATTN: Customer Care Center 8899 East 56th Street Indianapolis, IN 46249-3300	888-332-7411	http://www.dfas.mil/
Department of Defense	National Personnel Record Center	1 Archives Drive St. Louis, Missouri 63138	314-801-0800	http://www.archives.gov/st-louis/military-personnel/
Department of the Army	Information about reporting a death and benefits			http://myarmybenefits.us.army.mil/
Department of the Navy	Information about reporting a death and benefits			http://www.public.navy.mil/bupers-npc/support/casualty/SBP/Pages/default.aspx

156 | Resources

SOURCE	PURPOSE	ADDRESS	PHONE	WEBSITE
Gold Star Wives of America	Spouses of military members killed in action.	200 N. Glebe Road Rm 425 Arlington, VA 22203-3755	888-751-6350	www.goldstarwives.org
Headquarters U.S. Marine Corps	Service and Survivor Benefit Plan related questions	Henderson Hall, Arlington, Virginia	703-614-7171	http://www.hqmc.marines.mil/
Military Funeral Honors	Aid & Assistance to survivors		866-826-3628	https://www.dmdc.osd.mil/mfh/
Military.gov	Information about military survivor benefits			http://www.military.com/benefits/survivor-benefits/the-survivor-benefit-plan-explained.html
National Cemetery Administration	Military and veterans burial benefits and monument medallions		800-827-1000	http://www.cem.va.gov/
National Military Family Association	Aid & Assistance to surviving spouses	3601 Eisenhower Avenue, Suite 425 Alexandria, VA 22304	800-260-0218	www.nmfa.org
Navy-Marine Corps Relief Society	Aid & Assistance to surviving spouses	875 N. Randolph St. Suite 225 Arlington, VA 22203	800-654-8364	www.nmcrs.org
Society of Military Widows	Aid & Assistance to surviving female spouses		800-842-3451	www.militarywidows.org
Tragedy Assistance Program for Survivors	Aid & Assistance for surviving spouses	3033 Wilson Boulevard, Suite 630 Arlington, VA 22201	800-959-8277	www.taps.org
Veteran's Benefits Administration	VA related questions and benefits		800-827-1000	http://www.va.gov/

SOURCE	PURPOSE	ADDRESS	PHONE	WEBSITE
Veterans Group Life Insurance	Questions related to military and veterans insurance policies		800-419-1473	https://iris.custhelp.com/app/answers/detail/a_id/1703
Veterans of Foreign Wars (VFW)	Member benefits, assistance, & insurance	406 W. 34th St, Kansas City, MO 64111	816-756-3390	https://www.vfw.org/
Viet Nam Veterans of America	Member related questions	8719 Colesville Rd, Ste 100, Silver Spring, Md 20910	301-585-4000	http://vva.org/
Workers' Compensation office	Possibly work-related death benefits			

GENEALOGY

FAMILY MEMBERS

Here is a brief overview of my family members, including past spouses and their contact information (for notification purposes), step- and half- brothers and sisters and children. Please check the **NOTES** section at the end of this book for information about other possible family members.

Grandparents—Paternal

Grandfather: ....

Birthplace: ....

Birthdate: ....

Date/Place of death: ....

Grandmother (including maiden name): ....

Birthplace: ....

Birthdate: ....

Date/Place of death: ....

Address/Phone/Email: ....

....

Step-Grandparents—Paternal

Step-Grandfather: ....

Birthplace: ....

Birthdate: ....

Date/Place of death: ....

Step-Grandmother (including maiden name): ....

Birthplace: ....

Birthdate: ....

Date/Place of death: ....

Address/Phone/Email: ....

....

Grandparents—Maternal

Grandfather: ....

Birthplace: ....

Birthdate: ....

Date/Place of death: ....

Grandmother (including maiden name): ....

Birthplace: ....

Birthdate: ....

Date/Place of death: ....

Address/Phone/Email: ....

....

Step-Grandparents—Maternal

Step-Grandfather: ....

Birthplace: ....

Birthdate: ....

Date/Place of death: ....

Step-Grandmother (including maiden name): ....

Birthplace: ....

Birthdate: ....

Date/Place of death: ....

Address/Phone/Email: ....
....

Parents

Father: ....

Birthplace: ....

Birthdate: ....

Date/Place of death: ....

Mother (including maiden name): ....

Birthplace: ....

Birthdate: ....

Date/Place of death: ....

Address/Phone/Email: ....
....

Step- /Adoptive Parents

Step- /Adoptive Father: ....

Birthplace: ....

Birthdate: ....

Date/Place of death: ....

Step- /Adoptive Mother (including maiden name): ....

Birthplace: ....

Birthdate: ....

Date/Place of death: ....

Address/Phone/Email: ....

....

Siblings

Brother/Sister's name: ....

Birthplace: ....

Birthdate: ....

Date/Place of death: ....

Address/Phone/Email: ....

....

Parent's Names (if different from mine): ....

Brother/Sister's name: ....

Birthplace: ....

Birthdate: ....

Date/Place of death: ....

Address/Phone/Email: ....

....

Parent's Names (if different from mine): ....

Brother/Sister's name: ....

Birthplace: ....

Birthdate: ....

Date/Place of death: ....

Address/Phone/Email: ....

....

Parent's Names (if different from mine): ....

Brother/Sister's name: ....

Birthplace: ....

Birthdate: ....

Date/Place of death: ....

Address/Phone/Email: ....

....

Parent's Names (if different from mine): ....

Brother/Sister's name: ....

Birthplace: ....

Birthdate: ....

Date/Place of death: ....

Address/Phone/Email: ....

....

Parent's Names (if different from mine): ....

Brother/Sister's name: ....

Birthplace: ....

Birthdate: ....

Date/Place of death: ....

Address/Phone/Email: ....

....

Parent's Names (if different from mine): ....

Current Marriage or Partnering

Spouse/Significant Other (including maiden name)

Name: ....

Birthplace: ....

Birthdate: ....

Date of marriage/commitment: ....

Place of marriage/commitment: ....

Address/Phone/Email: ....

....

Previous Marriage(s)/Partnering(s)

First spouse/Significant other (including maiden name)

Name: ....

Birthplace: ....

Birthdate: ....

Date of marriage/commitment: ....

Place of marriage/commitment: ....

Address/Phone/Email: ....

Second spouse's /Significant other (including maiden name)

Name: ....

Birthplace: ....

Birthdate: ....

Date of marriage/commitment: ....

Place of marriage/commitment: ....

Address/Phone/Email: ....
....

Third spouse/Significant other (including maiden name)

Name: ....

Birthplace: ....

Birthdate: ....

Date of marriage/commitment: ....

Place of marriage/commitment: ....

Address/Phone/Email: ....
....

Children/Step-Children

Child's name: ....

Birthplace: ....

Birthdate: ....

Parent's Names: ....

Address/Phone/Email: ....
....

Date/Place of death: ....

Child's name: ....

Birthplace: ....

Birthdate: ....

Parent's Names: ....

Address/Phone/Email: ....

....

Date/Place of death: ....

MY MEMORIES

Throughout my life, I have many fond memories or family, friends, events and experiences. I thought I would share some of these with you … (See **NOTES** for any additional memories).

My earliest favorite life memory (and why):

What/Who inspired me the most (and why):

....

....

....

....

....

An achievement that I am most proud of is (and why):

....

....

....

....

One thing that I wish I had achieved or done better is (and why):

....
....
....
....

I wish I would have known when I would die so that I could have:

....
....
....
....

My favorite movie is (and why):

....
....
....
....

My favorite song is (and why):

....
....
....
....

My favorite book is (and why):

....
....
....
....

My favorite car is (and why):

....
....
....
....

If I had hit the lottery, I would have done the following with the money (and why):

....
....
....
....

My favorite quote/saying is (and why):

....
....
....
....

The thing I most regret in life is (and why):

....
....
....
....

The thing(s) that made me the happiest in my life is/are (and why):

....
....
....
....

The thing that I most hope happens in the future is (and why):
....
....
....
....

My favorite place (and why):
....
....
....
....
....

My fondest memory with my current spouse or significant other and why:
....
....
....
....

My fondest memory with my children as a group (and why):
....
....
....
....

My fondest memory with my son/daughter (and why):
....
....
....
....

My fondest memory with my son/daughter (and why):
....
....
....
....

My fondest memory with my son/daughter (and why):
....
....
....
....

My fondest memory with my son/daughter (and why):
....
....
....
....

My fondest memory of my father (and why):
....
....
....
....

My fondest memory of my mother (and why): ....
....
....
....
....

My fondest memory with my sister/brother (and why):
....
....
....
....

My fondest memory with my sister/brother (and why):
....
....
....
....

My fondest memory of my paternal grandfather (and why):
....
....
....
....

My fondest memory of my paternal grandmother (and why):
....
....
....
....

My fondest memory of my maternal grandfather (and why):
....
....
....
....

My fondest memory of my paternal grandmother (and why):

....

....

....

....

Other fond memories:

Use the **NOTES** pages to leave additional thoughts, advice, memories, or messages to family and special friends.

....

....

....

....

....

....

....

....

....

....

....

....

....

....

....

APPENDIX

GLOSSARY OF TERMS

401(k). A qualified retirement plan established by an employer that permits employees to invest part of their income into it without paying federal taxes until the money is withdrawn. Employers often match the employee contributions on a percentage basis.

Annuity. A form of insurance that pays someone a set amount of money each year.

Annuitant. A person named in a specialized insurance plan to receive payments or benefits.

Automatic bill payments. Money authorized by an account holder to be electronically transferred from their brokerage, banking or mutual fund account on scheduled dates for recurring debt payments.

Bank notes (also known as promissory notes). Negotiable financial instruments that are made by a bank and paid to the bearer on demand.

Beneficiary. A person named in a will, life insurance policy, retirement plan, pension, trust, or other revenue source to receive money or other advantage.

Bond. A financial instrument issued by a person, organization or government in order to raise money. It offers a guaranteed financial return by a specified date to those who purchase.

Burial plot. A section of ground in a cemetery designated for one or more graves.

Certified Financial Planner. A professional who has met specific certification criteria and is responsible for creating financial plans for clients. Examples of services provided include counseling on planning for retirement, insurance, taxes, business succession planning, investments, cash flow, and estates.

Certificate of Deposit (CD). A savings certificate that has a fixed interest rate and maturity date with access to funds restricted until it matures.

Credit reporting agency (also known as a credit bureau). A company that collects information from different sources and creates consumer credit reports used for a variety of purposes.

Creditor. A person or organization owed money by another individual or group.

Cremation. A process of combustion through which a body is reduced to ashes. It may follow a funeral or memorial and is an alternative to burial.

Crematory. A facility where bodies are cremated.

Crypt or niche. A chamber or vault used as a burial place.

Death Benefit. Proceeds paid to a beneficiary from an insurance policy, retirement plan or other source.

Death certificate. An official document signed by a physician and registered with the state in which death occurs, listing the date, cause and place of death.

Decedent or Deceased. Someone who has died.

Dividends. Periodic payments made by corporations to distribute a percentage of profits to shareholders who have invested in the company.

Durable Power of Attorney. A document authored by a grantor, principal, or owner that that names another person or someone to handle all medical or legal matters, business, private affairs for someone who is incapacitated or unable to handle his or her own affairs or make decisions.

Email username address. Information used by POP3 server to locate an email recipient for message delivery.

Employer Identification Number (EIN) (also known as Taxpayer Identification Number [TIN]). Unique nine-digit number issued by the Internal Revenue Service (IRS) to corporations, sole proprietors, partnerships and other business entities operating in the United States.

Errors and Omissions insurance (EO). Professional liability insurance (PLI), also called professional indemnity insurance (PII) but more commonly known as errors & omissions (E&O) in the US, is a form of liability insurance that helps protect professional advice- and service-providing individuals and companies from bearing the full cost of defending against a negligence claim made by a client, and damages awarded in such a civil lawsuit.

Eulogy. Speech or written document read that praises a deceased person at a funeral.

Executor or Executrix (also known as a legal representative). The man or woman assigned in a will to oversee the distribution of assets. This person has fiduciary responsibility to ensure that all assets dispersed are done in compliance with the stipulations of a last will and testament of a deceased person and existing law.

Flush ground grave marker. Flat grave memorial made of stone or metal and typically engraved with the occupant's vital information.

Fraternal organization. A type of social organization in which members with common interests and beliefs network for professional or social purposes. Examples are Daughters of the American Revolution, Lions Club, Masons, American Legion, Veterans of Foreign Wars and college fraternities.

Funeral Service. Ceremony held with the body of the deceased present to remember, honor, and respect the person who has died. The format varies and follows the wishes of the deceased or family members. It is in line with established cultural and religious standards, beliefs and practices. The coffin may be open or closed.

Grief Counselor. Person who practices a type of psychotherapy focused on helping survivors cope with grief and mourning following the death of a loved one.

Heirloom. A valuable object that has been passed down for generations in a family.

Incoming mail server (also known as an email server). An electronic device that connects from a client's computer to their Internet Service Providers server to collect electronic mail messages that have been sent to the client's email address. One form of this device is known as a Post Office Protocol version 3 (POP3) server.

Individual Retirement Account (IRA). Savings account that is set up by an employer or self-employed person to accrues assets for an employee's retirement.

Internet Protocol (IP) address. A unique number assigned to identify every computer connected to the Internet or a local area network (LAN).

Internet Service Provider (ISP). Company that provides computerized servers and equipment which allows clients to exchange email messages with others across the Internet and to search the Internet for information.

Internment. The act of burial.

Keogh Plan. A retirement plan for self-employed workers.

Last will and testament. A legal document created by someone to express how he or she wishes property and valuables to be distributed or handled after his or her death. It is normally administered by an Executor or Executrix or legal representative.

Layperson. A person not ordained by a religious organization or without particular qualifications or specialized knowledge in a given profession.

Licensing fee. An amount of money paid a government, organization or person for the privilege of doing something or using intellectual materials, products or services available.

Living Will (DNR). An advance directive completed by someone. It details the creator's desires for medical treatment when they are incapacitated or no longer able to make decisions related to their care. A typical stipulation is a "do not resuscitate" clause directing that all medical or artificial means of prolonging life be withheld.

Mail servers. Computerized devices located at an Internet Service Provider (ISP) site or at a company's own location. Incoming and outgoing email messages are processed through them. These devices perform a similar function to a post office that receives and processes incoming and outgoing letters and packages.

Mausoleum. A free-standing building used as a burial place.

Healthcare power of attorney (also known as a Living Will). A legal document that authorizes another person to make decisions regarding healthcare and medical treatment in the event the designator becomes incapacitated or is unable to consciously make decisions.

Memorial Service. A service held without the remains of someone who has died present. It is often held within a week of someone dying and is a more informal occasion where friends and family honor the deceased and celebrate his or her life.

Military discharge. Process of releasing a military member from additional service. Examples of this include, conclusion of contractual obligation, attainment of retirement age, due to a medical condition, or for poor performance or violation of the Uniform Code of Military Justice.

Military serial or service number. Used by the U.S. military branches from 1918 to 1969-1974 (depending on the branch of service) to identify service members. Following that time, social security numbers were used until June 2011. At that time, military branches began to again issue service numbers instead of social security numbers to help thwart identity theft, since these numbers appear on military identification (ID) cards.

Nuptial agreement. A written contract entered into before or after a couple marries or enters into a civil union. It is normally notarized and stipulates how assets and affairs will be settled in the event of separation or divorce.

Obituary. A published notice of death with a short personal biography of a deceased person.

Organ Donor. A person who voluntarily donates his or her body, organs, or tissue for scientific research and medical purposes. Families often donate in memory of their deceased loved one to save the lives of others.

Outgoing mail server. An electronic device used by an Internet Service Provider (ISP) to collect outgoing client email messages from its clients and transmit them via the Internet to other ISPs.

Pallbearer. One of several people who carry the coffin of a deceased person.

Password. Secret strings of letters, numbers and characters created to protect personal information on computers and log into accounts on the Internet.

Payee. Someone to whom money will be paid via a check, electronic money transfer, money order or through other means.

Personal Identification Number (PIN). Code required by banks, credit unions and other organizations to verify that a user's Automated Teller Machine (ATM) or online website login is valid before allowing access to an account.

Post Office Protocol, version 3 (POP3) server. Incoming mail servers that store sent and received messages on a local personal computer hard drive.

Probate. The legal process through which a last will and testament of a deceased person will be validated or proven as legitimate in a State court in order for an executor or executrix to settle an estate.

Profit sharing. A system in which employees receive a portion of the company's profits in addition to a salary.

Royalties. A percentage of income paid to an author, musician, inventor, artist, or composer for their work product.

Safe deposit box. A metal box, typically secured in a bank, where people store money, jewelry and other valuables along with important documents.

Savings Bond. A financial instrument issued by the U.S. Treasury with a specified dollar value, plus interest if it is held to the maturity date.

Simplified Employee Pension (SEP) Plan. A retirement plan set up by business owners to contribute to their own and their employee's retirement savings. Contributions are made to an Individual Retirement Account (IRA).

Simple Mail Transfer Protocol (SMPT) A type of mail server provided by an Internet Service Provider to transmit email information across the Internet to a client POP3 server for retrieval and storage.

Stockbroker (also known as an investment advisor). A commission-based, regulated professional who buys and sells stocks and securities over the counter or through a stock exchange.

Stock certificates. A document indicating ownership of one or more ownership shares in a company.

Survivor Benefits Plan (SBP). An insurance plan selected by a qualified retiree. It pays his or her surviving spouse and children, or in their absence another

"insurable interest" (e.g., business partner or parent), a monthly payment (annuity) to help supplement retirement income lost when the retiree dies.

Tax Sheltered Annuity (TSA); (aka 403b plan or 457b). Is a retirement plan for certain employees of public schools, employees of certain tax-exempt organizations, and certain ministers.

Thrift Savings Plan (TSP). A Federal government-sponsored retirement savings and investment plan established by Congress under the Federal Employees' Retirement System Act of 1986.

Trust. A legal arrangement in which a person or organization (e.g., bank) contracts to manage the money or property of someone else for a set period of time.

Upright grave marker comes in a variety of shapes, such as, rectangular, hearts, cross, praying hands or angel. They stand vertically above the ground and are inscribed with one or more occupant's names, dates of birth/death and often with an engraved message, photo or emblem.

Uniform Resource Locator (URL). Sometimes referred to as a Universal Resource Locator, it is the Internet address of a file or website consisting of a protocol (e.g., http://www.) followed by the name or address of a computer (e.g., robertwlucas.com) on a network that allows location of information.

Username (also called login/logon name, or sign-in/sign-on name). A unique set of numbers, letter and symbols designed to allow a computer user to access a computer system or online account information.

Veteran. A person who has served in any branch of the military.

Veterans Administration. A federal government agency responsible for administering benefits provided by law for military veterans.

Website domain. Names used in Uniform Resource Locators to identify particular sites or Web pages. For example in http://www.robertwlucas./com, robertwlucas.com is the domain name.

Website registrar. An organization responsible for managing Internet domain name reservations.

Appendix | 183

ADDITIONAL NOTES

ABOUT THE AUTHOR

As an internationally-known award-winning author, independent publisher, learning and performance expert, Robert (Bob) W. Lucas specializes in workplace performance-based training and consulting services and is Principal of *Robert W. Lucas Enterprises.* He has over four decades of experience in human resources development, management, and customer service in a variety of organizational environments and speaks to groups all over the country. Bob has served on various non-profit boards where he has been President of the Central Florida Chapter of the Association for Talent Development (formerly the American Society for Training and Development), Chair of Leadership Seminole in Seminole County, Florida and on the board for the Florida Authors and Publishers Association (FAPA).

Bob has spent most of his adult years learning the processes, procedures and skills necessary for dealing with people of all types and solving problems. He has researched and written on many topic areas related to the adult life cycle and the challenges people face in different phases of their life. He has put much of his knowledge to use to train people from all walks of life in various workplace and career situations. He has also conducted workshops for trainers who have taken their knowledge and skills back to share with new audiences.

In addition to being a performance consultant and trainer, Bob has written and contributed to thirty-seven books on a variety of workplace skills, relationship building and business development. He has the top-selling customer service textbook in the United States and has written hundreds of training leader guides, and support materials for several training videos.

Having served twenty-two years in the U.S. Marine Corps, personally survived a number of major medical events, and cared for two elderly parents, Bob is keenly aware of the need for financial and practical life planning. This recognition is the impetus for **The Survivor's Family Guide:** *A Resource for Loved Ones After Your Passing.* He continually stresses the need to plan in his workshops and

writings, and to his own family and friends. This book is a tool that he developed to help them and anyone else who will eventually have to deal with the loss of a loved one.

Bob earned a Bachelor of Science degree in Law Enforcement from the University of Maryland, an M.A degree with a focus in Human Resources Development from George Mason University and a second MA degree in Management and Leadership from Webster University.

CONTACT BOB LUCAS:
Phone: +1-407-695-5535 (United States)
Email: info@robertwlucas.com
Website: http://www.robertwlucas.com

BOOKS BY ROBERT W. LUCAS

All of the following books are available at your favorite book retailer and at http://www.robertwlucas.com.

- 231 Ways to Say I Love You … and Mean It
- Make Money Writing Books: Proven Profit-Making Strategies for Authors
- Please Every Customer: Delivering Stellar Customer Service across Cultures
- Energize Your Training: Creative Techniques to Engage Learners
- Customer Service Skills for Success
- Training Workshop Essentials: Designing, Developing and Delivering Learning Events That Get Results
- The Creative Training Idea Book: Inspired Tips & Techniques for Engaging and Effective Learning
- The BIG Book of Flip Charts
- How to be a Great Call Center Representative

"Grief is two parts. The first is loss. The second is the remaking of life.

Anne Roiphe

ORDER FORM
THE SURVIVOR'S FAMILY GUIDE

Cost (per copy – U.S. dollars)   Copies Ordered   Sub-Total
1 copy @ $18.95 each   _____   _____
2-10 @ $17.05 each   _____   _____
11-50 @ $13.25 each   _____   _____
51+   @ $ 11.35 each   _____
Recipients in Florida - add applicable:
State and local taxes   _____
Shipping/Handling   _____
                                TOTAL   _____

Shipping/Handling: 1–2 copies =$6.95

3 or more and international = based on weight (call/email before ordering)

Overnight Express and international delivery available at actual cost, plus $5.00.

.... Check here for express delivery

NOTE: Prices subject to change without notice.

Checks drawn on U.S. Banks in U.S. currency only and U.S. Postal Money Orders accepted.

Check/MO# ....enclosed

Ship To Address (No P.O. Boxes please):

....

....

Phone (with area code)..

Email:..

Mail To:
Robert W. Lucas Enterprises
1555 Pinehurst Drive, Casselberry, Florida 32707, USA
PH: +1-(407)695-5535. Email: info@robertwlucas.com

www.ingramcontent.com/pod-product-compliance
Lightning Source LLC
Chambersburg PA
CBHW080035120526
44588CB00035B/2403